JOURNAL MAGIC℠

Lessons in Therapeutic Writing

JOURNAL MAGIC℠

Lessons in Therapeutic Writing

Sue Meyn, M.C.

ISBN # 1-893171-03-5
Library of Congress Control Number: 200635453

This book is intended for educational purposes only and is not meant to be a substitute for the advice of qualified healthcare professionals.

Quotations used in this book are from volumes shown in the Bibliography at the back of the book.

Book Design, Cover Design: Paul McNeese
Cover Art: Chris LeCraw, Istockphoto.com
Editorial Supervision: Optimum Performance Associates, Chandler, AZ 85244-1764

Email: info@journalmagic.com
Online at: http://www.journalmagic.com

Printed in the United States of America

Table of Contents

Introduction to "JournalMagic"

This book contains just about everything you'll need to help you open the door, break through your resistances, and get started with your journal writing. An optional supplement to this book—a card set we call ***JournalMagic* JournalCards**—will assist you, and we'll tell you how to make the most of them.

The sooner you begin your writing life, the sooner you will discover the magic and power that you carry within. You will define the magic that appears in front of you as you write. It can show itself as venting—just releasing feelings and thoughts that have been bugging you, or as brainstorms that offer you meaningful insight and wisdom, or the magic may show itself to you in subtle patterns that you become aware of days or weeks later. You can be sure that you will find the magic . . . once you actually begin.

Please remember, your journal will reflect *you* perfectly and will not follow any formula—nor should it. The power of the journal lies in that fact—that it is a perfect reflection of you. It's impossible do it wrong. It can be a place where you have the opportunity to learn about the multifaceted being that you truly are! You are stepping into a new relationship with your *self*—one that can have a profound impact all your other relationships!

OPEN THE DOOR

One of the ways we know that personal writing is a popular activity is by looking at the shelves full of blank books in bookstores and gift shops. That notion is reinforced when we hear counselors, TV personalities and famous coaches coaxing us to "write it down."

When people ask me how to do journaling 'right', I tell them that however they do it *is* right. Apparently, that's hard to grasp in today's world, where almost everything is presented to us with a rulebook or user's guide. "Simply begin" is generally not viewed as adequate direction.

We commonly turn to experts to tell us the 'best' way to do something, but in this case, **you** are the expert about yourself. You have the freedom to express yourself as you who are and as you change from day to day, moment to moment. As you write about your life and the things that make you happy, angry, silly or sad you will be reflecting upon *your* life and writing *your* journal. Not hard at all. So let's quit lecturing and move on.

HERE WE GO!

Find the kind of book you most prefer—spiral bound, hardbound, fancy or simple. The pen you use is important, as well—unless, of course, you are using a computer to keep your journal. Whatever works best for you is what is correct.

Take a deep breath. Shake off expectations. Settle into a comfortable spot. Open up your journal.

Leave that front page blank—just to give anyone who might open it by mistake a chance to close it back up. *(Privacy is of primary importance!)* You may want to put your name in it, the date you are beginning, and whatever else you want.

Do you have a comfortable place to sit? By a table? Your journal in your lap? How about some tea? Want to light a candle? You get the idea—make this experience your own.

Breathe deeply again and allow yourself some time to just be quiet.

THE DATE!

Make it easy on yourself and begin first—and always—with the date. *This becomes important when you are looking back.*

SIMPLE QUESTION

You may have a place to start, so just go ahead. If you are hesitating and need a little help, then write a simple question at the top of the page, like, "What's going on?" Or "How do I feel?" We'll add in the *JournalCards* soon enough, but for now, just stay with a simple question.

SET A TIMER

To begin with, look at your watch or set a timer for about five minutes. Since most of us are so pressed for time in these busy days, it is wise to set a timer when you are new to journal writing. It is much easier to stop when you know that there is a time 'quota' you have fulfilled, and you will probably find it easier to begin when you know just how much time you have available to you. *This isn't a rule, by the way, just a suggestion.*

DON'T JUDGE

Begin to write now, not planning your sentences ahead, but just letting the words appear on the page, one at a time, as they flow from your insides, down your arm, and out through your pen. Remember that you are not trying to be profound and that your writing is only for you; no one else will see what you write (unless you choose to share). I often encourage people to pay more attention at first to the process of writing and less to the content. Really, you are learning to open and move into a flow.

DONE?

You are now a journal writer!
Yes, it really is that simple.

REVIEWING THE STEPS:

1. Find a private space that is peaceful for you, then take some time to quiet yourself and breathe gently.

2. Open the journal you have chosen to work with, and pick up your pen.

3. Date your entry and start with a simple question like, "What's going on?"

4. Write for about five minutes. Try setting a timer.

5. Don't judge or evaluate. Just keep going.

6. Be clear about this being your own private journal. *You share it only as you decide what is best for you.*

7. Be free of concern about spelling, punctuation, grammar, or penmanship.

ROAD BLOCKS AND RESISTANCES

Simple as this journaling may seem, many people find that personal issues pop up in front of them and stop them in their tracks. You may find that simply talking about them will help you to move past your own obstacles. Finding out that you are not alone may help, too. You may wish to write about your concerns and resistance, or you may feel that serious issues have come up that require the help of a trained counselor. Stay with it. It *is* worth it! *You are worth it!*

Lots of folks have been frightened about writing since their school days, when they had to compose essays—following the rules of grammar, using proper punctuation, spelling perfectly. We all learned to write our letters and compose our sentences early in our schooling. However, for many of us, it left *us*—our thoughts and feelings—out of the experience. G. Lynn Nelson addresses this issue in his book, **Writing and Being,** in which he shares his own discovery process, one that evolved as he began to journal and discovered the enormity of the feelings he had to express. That story is one that many of us can relate to. As school children, we were so busy in our heads (learning the rules) that we had no room to attend to our feelings or to discern what was important for us to express and write about at the time.

The journal gives you the chance to change all that. As the expert in your own life, *you decide* how you want to spell, if you want to punctuate or use 'proper' grammar. The idea is to be completely free to focus on your own expression. The more you practice this writing without rules, the more open you become to your ideas, your feelings, and your 'magic'. Later, should you later decide to turn some of your private writing into something public, you would, of course, alter it to conform to those standard rules of grammar.

Another roadblock that most of us encounter is the critic we carry within us, the one who likes to try to push us around and tell us how we are doing. Especially when we are beginners, the critic will try to stick its nose into our journals. The inner critic, who also likes to evaluate and judge what we do and say, is tied to the rule-following part of us, our left-brains—the linear, logical and orderly part of our minds. This left-brain carries ideas that we picked up as youngsters when our parents and teachers taught us how to follow the 'rules' about getting along in the world. Unfortunately, the left brain often gets out of hand and squelches us from expressing the very parts of ourselves—emotions and creative ideas--that most need to be expressed! Like our parents, the critic is well intentioned but needs to be quieted in order for us to open to richer aspects of ourselves.

With practice, your journal can help you to overcome the influence of that stubborn inner critic. Here's how. As we journal, since there are no rules, the critic can relax. This takes a little practice, since most of us are habitually on guard in most parts of our lives. As our critic relaxes, another part of our brain— the right brain—becomes engaged. The right brain holds our creativity, emotions and sense of fun. Eventually, we are able to express more from this creativity center. Then we are able to discover more and more of our own magic. The left brain, where the critic hangs out, finds out that the right brain has something important to share. Brain hemispheres begin to work more cooperatively—giving us more brainpower! So you can tell your critic to take a vacation when you work with your journal! Your creativity will expand as you bypass this menace to movement!

SAFETY

Part of what makes it possible to reach into our right brain and to let go of that left brain critic is knowing that what we write is for *our own eyes only*. If you share parts of what you have written, it must be only because you choose to. This is very important. Without this assurance of safety, you will not be able to dip into the unknown parts of your history, your dreams, and your imagination. You will not be able to let go of your critic, to move into your creativity, or to engage your special magic. This is an obstacle that *must* be avoided.

What other roadblocks have you encountered? The issue of someone else reading your journal was addressed above, but you may need to have a family meeting about privacy to ensure that safety. Are you concerned that writing it down "makes it real"? I would suggest experimenting with small issues at first, while you develop trust. You may even allow yourself to tear up what you have written. The important part is getting it out of you; keeping it isn't always necessary. Another resistance that many people encounter is fear of the blank page. Hopefully, this guide will help you to move beyond that.

I believe you will be able to move through any of the rough spots that may have emerged. Journaling offers wonderful opportunities to move into greater depth right away! If you still feel stuck, you may want to visit my Internet website, www.journalmagic.com and consider a session in Journal Coaching. It is a phone/email connection made to help you deal with current issues in your life using your journal as your assistant.

POWERFUL RESEARCH PROVES WHAT WE KNOW

There is no question that writing in a journal offers healing benefits. More than fifteen years of in-depth research by psychologist James Pennebaker supports that contention. He has shown that writing for as little as 15 minutes at a time for four days in a row tends to result in lowered blood pressure, enhanced immune system functioning, and fewer doctors office visits.

Later research, published in the Journal of the American Medical Association in 1999, suggests that arthritis and asthma patients who journaled just three days in a row, for 30 minutes at a time, experienced a measurable reduction in symptoms for up to four months. In both cases, participants were asked to write about difficult or traumatic life situations. It is important to write about the hard parts of life as well as the joyful ones. Remember, though, however *you* do it will be just right.

MORE QUESTIONS . . .

How often should I write in my journal?

Think about it as though you were creating a new friendship. How often do you want to connect when you are just getting acquainted? That could range from every day to once a week. Find your own range, but remember that it is both a habit and a relationship that you are working toward establishing. You will have to decide how important this relationship is to you. Greater frequency is usually better. And remember, you can write for just five minutes and still cover a lot of territory. Trust yourself to do what is best for you, and do your best to avoid self-criticism if you miss a few days. Just begin again.

Do I just sit down and write?

There are many valid techniques you can use to journal besides timed writing or free writing. Your *JournalCards* will give you dozens of suggestions, but there are a few *classics* that can be used repeatedly. Those will be thoroughly described in upcoming chapters. Please consult *Journal to the Self,* by Kathleen Adams, for more instructions on additional techniques. Kathleen is the "mama" of journal therapy and another great resource to consult. Her website is: www.journaltherapy.com.

JournalCards! What are they?

The *JournalCards* packet is a set of fifty-five different cards, each having a word, a picture, and four questions on them. They are meant to help jump-start your creative process. We have found that when they are used at the beginning of a journaling session, whether you are journaling alone or as a member of a group, they help to shift the focus—quickly and easily—from a 'normal' left-brained, logical approach to a whole-brain, *deeper* perspective. Because your own intuition picks each card, you will find that they often fit perfectly into the very topic you need to explore.

WHERE DID THEY COME FROM?

JournalCards were created to answer the primary complaint I heard from new journal writers, which was, "I don't know what to write about!"

You will find yourself responding to different parts of the cards each time you pick one. While a word may fit perfectly the issue that is most on your mind at one time, the picture may touch you in a special way another time. The four questions are meant to help you sift through your current thoughts so as to find a direction that is closest to where you want to go at the time. Different questions will fit better for different situations you may be going through.

I created these cards after years of enjoying *Runes* and *Medicine Cards* and *Inner Child Cards*. I find cards quick, accessible and fun. When a card is created in a positive way, it can help you to shift from a negative or unhealthy perspective to an attitude that empowers, uplifts, and offers guidance. That was certainly my intention as I created the *JournalCards.*

A LITTLE HISTORY

I have been a counselor for over 25 years and find the use of questions a way to help guide people toward discovering more of their own power, their inner gifts, or their personal magic—whatever one chooses to call it. We all need to learn how to ask our own questions, and the *JournalCards* offer a way to do that. It's like visiting with a counselor—after a few appointments, you may know *just* what they are going to ask. My hope is that as you use the cards your own questions will float to the surface. You will find yourself achieving great personal growth as you work with them. Sometimes, however, you may need more guidance than you can obtain from just writing. Those are the times when you may need an outside voice to help you. Of course, share your cards if and when you visit your counselor.

HOW TO USE JOURNALCARDS!

There is no right or wrong way to use the *JournalCards*. Certainly, we don't want to set up rules in a rule-less process, so allow the cards to speak to you according to your feelings in the moment. You can even go so far as to permit yourself to choose another card when you don't like the first one! *You* are the person who wants to create a richer and more complete relationship with yourself and those you love; so let the cards assist you in the "getting to know you" process.

ONE, TWO, THREE AND MORE

The most common way of using the cards is one at a time. Use one to open a journaling session or as the focus for one brief journaling entry. Remember to set a timer to give yourself some structure as you proceed. As you become more comfortable with the cards, use them as support in the midst of your journaling, as well. You may find yourself attending to one question—and you might then choose a card to offer you some "out of the box" perspective.

Another way to use a single *JournalCard* is at the end of a writing session. You could pull a card to help you summarize your feelings or to give you an idea to take along with you as you proceed through your day. You will find that a single card may also be useful in a discussion with a close friend or loved one. Even talking about ideas that spring from the cards can be meaningful and fun.

Two at a time is a way to start more gently, I've discovered, because then you can choose the one that feels most comfortable to write about. Often I have seen a card picked by someone that was so 'right on' that it was scary for the writer. Choosing two cards allows more choice and less fear. The two-card approach can also be used to explore a masculine or feminine perspective. Choose a card with the left hand for the feminine perspective and with the right hand for the masculine approach. Similarly, two can be used to exemplify any other polarity, such as selfish and selfless, parent and child, strong and vulnerable, and so on. Sounding like fun, right?

I personally love using the *JournalCards* in a series of three as I explore a particular question or concern I may have. The first card I pick represents the current situation in my life. The second card stands for an *Action Step* that would be useful to take in regard to that situation. The third shows us what the newly evolved situation could be if we take that recommended action.

This is a delightful and meaningful exercise. I can't think of a time when it was not deemed extremely useful in our local journaling groups. Sometimes it takes a little work to make the cards fit into an action or as part of a current concern, but my experience is that if we stay with it, something 'clicks' and we gain a new perspective.

➢ Current situation in my life;
➢ *Action Step* to take in regard to that situation;
➢ Newly created scenario after action has been taken.

FIVE AT A TIME!

When I do retreats and workshops, I often suggest a longer exercise that uses five cards. The first one represents something that is no longer of concern in one's life. The second card is about the current situation, followed by the *Action Step* in the third, the new situation with the fourth, and the fifth is something that will show up in the near future. It's another fun way to explore where one is and where one may be going.

- Something that is no longer of concern;
- Current situation in my life;
- *Action Step* to take in regard to that situation;
- Newly created scenario after action has been taken; and
- Something coming in the near future.

Because these cards are full of questions and not answers, you will find yourself drawing more and more deeply from your inner wisdom, your inner healer, and your more profound creative spirit. The cards offer general direction, which you will make specific to yourself.

This IS magic, but it is YOUR magic!

You are the person who will pick the card that fits for you, and you will determine how much accuracy and power you want to give to your choices.

Some people may choose to use these cards simply as writing prompts, with no special personal meaning attached. That, too, is an excellent way to use them. One friend said she would use them to help her write her speeches, and another has reported that they helped her with topics for English classes and creative writing classes.

MAKE YOUR OWN

In the classes I teach, I suggest that people create their own cards. Obviously, the style is simple, and I do believe that we need to learn to take responsibility for asking our own questions about our lives. You can use a computer to create them or just cut and paste. Standard index cards (3x5 inches) are just the size. Get a group together and have each person create several cards. When they are completed, you can copy them and provide a whole new creative set for yourselves! Explore all kinds of prompts—from pictures to quotes to advertising slogans. You will be surprised at how creative you are! This activity will help you remember even more that *you are the magic maker in your life!*

Your Finished Journals

Many people have asked me what to do with journals that are filled. My response is usually, "What do you *want* to do with them?" In a medium with no rules, there are unlimited ways to manage your journals. Some journalers keep them to refer to later as a source of strength as they go though difficult life events. Some destroy them. Some read through them to discover patterns to appreciate or to change about themselves. Others use them as a reference to use for creative writing, and some people just like to maintain their own history to pass down to their family. I can also refer you to a book, ***Harvesting Your Journals,*** by Rosalie Deer Heart, for more ideas about how to use your finished epistles.

My belief in this medium is that it is a wonderful way to grow and change as an individual. I have done a little of all of the above, and I continue to expect to find still more ways l to explore with them. I trust you to find your own beliefs and your own feelings about these special friends, your journals.

What else?

This introduction is intended to be a brief guide to beginning your journal writing process. You may yet have more questions. Feel free to contact me by e-mail for additional help. Using the coaching approach, we can explore further into how you may best use your journal. For a great guide for more techniques you can use in journal writing, go to ***Journal to the Self,*** by my guide, Kathleen Adams, whom I mentioned earlier. There is also an **Online Journal Class** available through my website that guides you through sixteen techniques.

Celebrate!

I hope that you can enjoy the *"you"* that you find presented on your journal pages as they accumulate over the weeks and months ahead. I also predict that you will celebrate your life with more gusto as a result. As we are all now well aware, we never know what our futures hold. Let us all move forward, embracing life as best we can. May many blessings come as you move forward living, reflecting, and writing about your life!

Another Introduction

Hey! Good for you! You have made a commitment to take these classes to expose yourself to a wide range of journal writing techniques. You will be surprised at how well they help you to discover different parts of yourself—parts you may not have known about before. In addition, you will be encouraged to make journaling an ongoing habit in your life!

The following four lessons were first written several years ago. Many of the techniques come directly from the ***Journal to the Self*** certification program, with my own stamp put upon them. As you work them through, they will help you by outlining the basic techniques you will be using as you experience the upcoming projects.

Let's cover some basic guidelines before we go further:

> ➤ Each of the four lessons is geared to take you about 90 minutes. You can do them in more or less time, but for the greatest benefit it's a good idea to allow yourself the hour-and-a-half timeframe so you may go through the exercises without rushing.

> ➤ Some people will ONLY write their journal by hand, while others prefer to use the keyboard. You may even want to do some of both. Each has its advantages, so it is really a personal choice.

> ➤ You are creating a private relationship with your journal. You will decide if there are excerpts that you want to share, but first and foremost I want you to be secure that your journal is a private place just for you. That safety will help you to reach further within.

➢ Make note of your reactions and questions as you proceed through the lessons. Pay attention to what goes on for you, how you feel as you proceed through the techniques. Doing so may help to point you toward more questions, new themes, and ways to release.

➢ I suggest that you may want to continue to use the techniques learned in previous lessons so you can become more comfortable with them. Your responses will always be different!

➢ Please remember to enjoy yourself! There are no rules for journal writing----you do it as *you* choose. There are no requirements about spelling, penmanship, grammar or punctuation. This is *private* writing. Only if you choose to turn it into *public* writing you will need to concern yourself with those matters.

➢ Questions? Feel free to email me at any time if you are unclear about directions or have any other question or concerns about the Projects developed in this book; my e-mail address is *smeyn1@cox.net*. I want you to enjoy the discovery of your inner magic! *Special Note:* I want to once again acknowledge Kathleen Adams and her book, ***Journal to the Self***. By taking her certification program, I learned many new techniques, some of which I will share with you. More importantly, by attending Kay's workshops I was able to open up and allow myself to take journal writing more seriously. It was encouragement I needed and for which I will always be in her debt.

The Five Minute Sprint

The Five Minute Sprint is a great technique, one that you will repeat over and over in various forms. What makes this technique so valuable is that it is **timed**.

For many of us, writing in our journals sounds like something that will take a lot of time—and most of us don't have a lot of time. This technique bypasses all that. It says simply, "Open your journal, set your timer, and just write for five minutes."

Easy. Direct. Simple. For today's purposes use this topic: if you have already been a journal keeper, write on **"My joys and frustrations with journal writing"**, or if you are a beginner, use the title **"My greatest joys and worst fears about keeping a journal"**.

Literally, set a timer or note the time on your clock as you begin. What you say is much less important than your experience of doing a time-limited writing piece.

GO!
(DON'T READ FURTHER UNTIL
YOU HAVE DONE THE SPRINT.)

In almost every session throughout this book, we will begin with a **Five Minute Sprint**. For one thing, it allows you to *gently* let go of what's going on outside you and begin to move inward. Sometimes it's hard to let go of external issues and move inside, but it is part of the balance that most of us need. If we put it off because "there isn't enough time", we may never begin.

The **Five Minute Sprint** is a good technique when you are feeling stressed, upset or anxious. In just a few minutes you can discharge the essence of your concerns and have more "room" for making decisions and taking action.

Next, try another **Five Minute Sprint**, this time asking yourself, "Are there any concerns or worries going on that are distracting me from moving ahead with more sureness in my life right now? What are they?"

Once again, set your timer and

GO!

So, how does that feel? Are you surprised at what you wrote or how much you wrote? Take a few minutes just to process your brief experience with this technique.

Just for fun, read one of your **Sprints** out loud (to yourself). How do you feel when you do that? As you go through your week, try doing a **Five Minute Sprint** several different times during the day just to get the feel for it. You may even find it a ritual you want to maintain.

You can decide what fits best for you in terms of continuing on. There will be three more techniques offered in this lesson. You can stop here or go on; it's up to you.

Clustering

This technique is one that is particularly helpful when you are trying to pull a lot of different ideas together. It is essentially a brainstorming technique.

Here's how it goes. You begin with a word or phrase that you want to explore more deeply. Let's say you are looking at your most positive personal characteristics (Hey, might as well build self-esteem at the same time!). You will write the phrase "**Positive Personal Characteristics**" in the center of a blank piece of paper.

POSITIVE
PERSONAL
CHARACTERISTICS

Then you will draw a circle around it.

POSITIVE
PERSONAL
CHARACTERISTICS

From the circle, you will draw a line—at random—and then write the first word or phrase that comes to mind, like "friendly." You then circle that word.

(Diagram on following page)

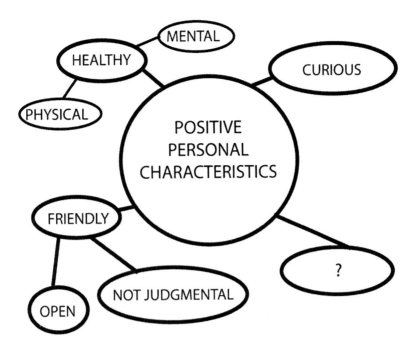

If you want to add another characteristic related to FRIENDLY, draw a line from that circle and write it, then circling that word. If you want to simply write an unrelated positive trait, then you draw another line from the main circle, write the word and circle it.

Continue in this vein until you cannot think of anything else to write. Then stay with it a few minutes longer allowing other thoughts or images to emerge. As with all brainstorming you are to censor nothing. All ideas have equal value. Write down whatever comes to mind and don't judge what you have written.

Part of what makes **Clustering** so valuable is that it encourages you to use both your right and left brain hemispheres. You write down words—a *left-brain* function—but you are also creating a pattern, which activates the *right brain*. As both sides of your brain operate simultaneously and interactively you are more likely to come up with creative ideas that you wouldn't be able to connect with if you were just writing a regular list. **Clustering** *is a whole-brain exercise.*

Because you begin to create a kind of picture as you do this exercise, you can have new thoughts or images appearing as you see trends or patterns. This could be referred to as an "Aha" experience, in which something new jumps out at you from the **Cluster.** I have a simple example of this. I did a cluster one day when I was feeling a bit upset. I wrote the word SELF in the center of the page and circled it. I then wrote a string of words that were connected with lines—TIRED, UNINSPIRED, FRUSTRATED and SMALL.

As I wrote, I knew that these words represented only my present experience, so I began expanding my view of my "self". Soon I had the whole page covered, and I could see that I was *much* more than those first few limiting words. It was a revelation that helped me to completely flip my mood at the time.

After you have written your **Cluster**, take a few moments to write about what you learned. You don't want to lose your whole-brain view, and you may have trouble recreating the experience, so it's important to record your discoveries. You may have had great insights, or you may have been pointed toward another word or phrase that would better describe your current dilemma. Whatever you discover, write it down just below your **Cluster**.

So, enough talk. Get your blank piece of paper ready, pick a word or phrase that you want to **Cluster** (*Positive Personal Characteristics*) and begin. *Allow yourself about eight to ten minutes.*

GO!

Again, make note of what you liked and didn't like about this technique. Some folks love it and others hate it. And that's part of the idea of this basic course—to allow you to have the opportunity to 'taste' lots of different techniques and find which ones work best for you.

Try putting into words how you think **Clustering** can help you. Think about situations where this kind of brainstorming could be useful. You might even want to go so far as to make a small list of situations where you can imagine using clustering.

The hardest part of this exercise is deciding just what to put into the center of the page. If it isn't 'juicy' enough you won't have enough ideas to carry you.

This technique is also called **Mind Mapping,** so named in books on the subject by Tony Buzan. ***Writing the Natural Way***, by Gabrielle Lusser Rico, describes using the cluster to improve one's creative writing. So you may want to go to your library or bookstore to look for this and other books.

I'd suggest that you build another **Cluster** right now, before you move on, perhaps putting in the middle an emotion you have been feeling lately. Explore!

Favorite People

This technique is one of my favorites and can be used in a variety of ways. The easiest and most obvious is simply to pick someone who is very dear and important to you. Once you have them identified in your own mind, sit back, relax, and just read through the rest of the instructions!

This is an exercise that involves the use of descriptive words. For all would-be writers, it assists in the necessary developmental process of creating word pictures. For journal writers, it is more an opportunity to blend into the experience and pull up as many meaningful words of description as you can to express the thoughts and feelings you have inside. As you go through the process, you will find your awareness increasing. As you proceed with this technique, you may even find that you have more writing talent than you realized!

First, write on your paper the name of the person you want to describe. Then put your pen down and read through the following guided meditation. (Or have someone read it to you, which will allow you relax completely, close your eyes, and really be there!)

✦ Meditation ✦

Relax, allow your eyes to soften . . . Take a nice deep breath . . .
Let yourself soften into this experience . . . Take another
cleansing breath . . . and another. Now, imagine your mind as
a movie screen. See your special person coming toward you
from the distance. You can see this person more clearly the
closer he/she comes . . . You see things you never noticed before.
You take in the hair color, eye color, clothing and even the walk
. . . nothing escapes your awareness as you practically breathe
them in . . . Now shift your awareness away from them and
into yourself . . . Notice how you feel being close to this person.
You notice what goes on in your own body as your special
person moves toward you and then gives you his/her full
attention . . . And then you once again take your attention back
to your friend . . . Remember why this person is so special . . .
You can see beyond their physical being into their very soul . . .
Enjoy this time you have with this very significant person, and
stay there as long as you like . . . and when you are ready, open
your eyes, take a gentle breath, and begin to write about your
"favorite person."

You can go as long as you want, but we suggest that you keep it at less than 15 minutes.

GO!

So, how do you feel? Please take some time and write about what that experience was like for you—what you liked or didn't like. How do you feel about what you wrote? *You may want to read it aloud—or even find someone to read it to.*

This technique works nicely with other people, with alter egos, historical figures, fictional characters for a novel, or simply the people we live with day in and day out. In later sessions, we will use this technique in combination with others, and it can help to evoke even more personal power.

Doing **Favorite People** can be a memorable way to honor another person for a holiday—in a card or in a frame with a picture. Once you have written it several times, your own creative ideas will emerge!

Ready to move on? Or do you want to go back and do another **Favorite People**?

Asking Questions

The last technique for this lesson is less well defined. *It is about asking the questions necessary to dig into yourself, your life and your experiences.* As a therapist, it is what I need to do best, to help folks come to new self-awareness, which is a building block of healing. In this process of writing, too, questioning is important as you seek increased awareness and more personal discoveries.

In journal writing, we often act as our own guides, so it is important to have some idea about how to come up with the questions to ask. I believe that as we are bombarded by the electronic media and because we are often spoon-fed with information, our powers of questioning have been weakened. Additionally, if we don't focus with questions and statements as we write, there can be a tendency to drift from one thought to another without successfully reaching the 'depths' we desire.

Some journalers simply complain that they just don't know what to write about. I hear many complaints about staring at an empty page. To help people overcome this block, Kathleen Adams created a series of questions or statements that she called ***Springboards***. There are times when you need to refer to a 'cheat sheet' of ideas to help you get going. This was one reason I created

JournalCards—to help give suggestions for topics to write about. *JournalCards* can help you to remember how to ask meaningful questions.

For now, my suggestion is to consider these aspects of your life:

- ➤ *Home*
- ➤ *Relationships*
- ➤ *Work*
- ➤ *Play*
- ➤ *Friends*

- ➤ *Spirituality*
- ➤ *Vacations*
- ➤ *Conflict*
- ➤ *Health*
- ➤ *Money*

With this list in mind, make up a question that would be good for you to consider in regard to each topic.

Here's an example: **"What can I do, today, to brighten my home?"**

Take each word from the list and make one question that would help you to stay more aware of what's important in your current life. And why not add words to the list that mean something to you? Make questions or statements about them.

As you go about your day, notice the kinds of questions you ask yourself, like, "What's so important about that?" or "What am I doing?" Those, too, can be useful when you are journaling.

What's important within all this is to be aware that we can *always* have a question to ask ourselves. We may even ask, "What question would be most productive for me to ask right now?"

Once you have begun your list of words and questions, put them on a separate piece of paper and stick them in the back of your journal for those times when you come up blank. As you move through your journal, other questions and topic areas will come up. Put a star next to them so that you can go back later and add them to your list. With your list of questions you can also keep pictures, quotes, photos and whatever else you can imagine. They are all grist for the mill.

Just to round out your experience, take one of your questions and write it down. Then, set your timer and do another **Five Minute Sprint**.

Enjoy!

True to my word, I will ask you to start your class with a **Five Minute Sprint**. I find that it is important to do this in order to make the transition from being involved with the world outside of me to the world inside of me.

Let this be the topic for your **Five Minute Sprint**: "What issues are rattling around in my head or causing me pressure in my life that I need to let go of or set aside in order to be more present?"

That may be a little unwieldy, but you get the picture. What is going on in your life right now that may be distracting you from turning within and being fully present?

Set your timer for five minutes and just write. (Remember, no planning, censoring, trying to make it 'sound good'. Just be yourself and let whatever you have to say just *flow*.)

GO!

Timed Writing – Planner Book Entries

So, you already know about **Five Minute Sprint**s and how valuable it can be to write for just those few minutes. I want to expand on that some. In truth, it is valuable to set a timer or have an idea of how long you want to write whenever you sit down to journal.

One of the biggest issues I encounter as I teach classes and talk with people about journaling is the issue of *time*. How do I fit in time for myself? How can I do journaling when I don't have time for other chores in my daily life?

These are realistic concerns and for that reason, you may want to allow yourself only five or ten or fifteen minutes *any time* you write in your journal.

Beyond that, there is a distinct advantage to writing for a certain amount of time *because the time becomes a kind of container*. It is as though you are filling a container with words and when it is full you know it is time to move on. Using timed boundaries just keeps your writing in check. Even though writing is good for us in general, when we go on and on in an unfocused and unproductive way, it can help to keep us stuck rather than moving on.

Kathleen Adams worked in a psychiatric hospital for some time and there made the discovery that unless there is a sense of containment for the writing, it can add to—rather than decrease—the anxiety and sense of confusion within the writer. When there is a boundary of time created at the beginning, one knows when one is finished, and that can support a sense of growth and accomplishment.

Tristine Rainer, in her book, **The New Diary**, says, "Using the diary effectively depends only upon the degree to which you trust your intuition and your process. The very act of sitting down with the diary signifies a readiness to commune with the self; and the very act of writing may place you inside the mystery of self-healing and self-recreation, no matter what is written or how it is expressed."

So you can see that what is important is less a matter of how long you write and more a matter of your *intention* when you sit down to write. Therefore, I am suggesting that before you write anything, *you* decide what is appropriate for you at the time. No matter what technique you may use, always consider how much time you want to spend. This will make all your writing more defined and manageable.

In addition to timing your writing, there is another effective way of journaling within the confines of your daily routine. Most busy people today use some kind of planner or calendar. It is possible to flip from one page to the next of your calendar, and doing so will bring back very specific memories of things that you did, people you saw, and even feelings that you had. The planner is, indeed, a kind of journal or diary; it reflects your life back to you.

My suggestion is that you consider some quick ways that you can journal right in your planner—especially on those days when you can find *no time* to write in your regular journal. Write a single word that describes your mood. Draw faces that describe how you feel about various parts of your day. Write questions that you want to pursue when you have more time for your regular journal. Or write yourself a note, put it on a sticky, telling yourself what a wonderful person you are!

To practice this technique, get your planner out and look through it. Notice what an effective journal it is by flipping through a few pages, noting how it immediately helps you to 'see' what that week was about. Consider what few words you could add to it that would give you more of the benefits of journaling. Let it be a place to 'dump' a few words, offer yourself support or just a place to describe the good and the rough parts of your day. This is a good way to fill in the holes from your regular journal (or to begin your writing habit). It's also another place to keep track of questions you want to pursue further.

Steppingstones

Now for a change of pace: **Steppingstones** is a technique developed by Ira Progoff, the father of journal therapy and a leading proponent of the psychological-spiritual use of journal writing. He practiced depth psychology and used the journal as the method to help us each move into our greater wisdom. **Steppingstones** involves identifying those important steps we have taken that have helped us get to where we are now in our lives. They always begin with:

1. "I was born…"

Usually, the important steps in our lives can be summed up in eight to 12 steps, regardless of the specific topic we may be exploring. When you write your **Steppingstones** it is not necessary that they be in chronological order; just let them emerge for you one at a time. Don't think too hard; just let those life-changing moments come to you, one at a time. You needn't write more than a phrase about each as they spring into your mind.

Steppingstones are useful for getting 'the big picture' of your life. We can look at our lives in many different ways, so there may be many different kinds of **Steppingstones** that we might address. For instance, you may want to focus on your educational development, or your history with relationships, with food, with friends, with money. There are hundreds of aspects of your life that you can explore.

What I want you to do for this time is simply to look at your life and what has happened that has gotten you to where you are now. There is no value of 'good' or 'bad' attached to these experiences; they just *are.* They give you an overview of your life. My own **Steppingstones** today look like this:

1. *I was born.*
2. *I went off to school reluctantly, being very shy.*
3. *I started clarinet lessons and played through junior and senior high school.*
4. *I went away to college and loved it.*
5. *I met and married my husband.*
6. *I graduated from college and had two children.*

7. *I got divorced and two years later my ex-husband died in an accident.*

8. *I went to graduate school.*

9. *I worked as a counselor for many years.*

10. *I remarried.*

11. *I began exploring creative expression and teaching on my own and in community colleges.*

That is an example of **Steppingstones**. They are usually short and to the point. Allow yourself now to do your own **Steppingstones**. They will take you only a few minutes to jot down. Just *allow* them to emerge one at a time. (Know too that what appears for you today may be very different from what you write about a week from now, so there is no 'right' answer to come up with.)

GO!

Now that you have your own **Steppingstones** in front of you, I want you to look through them, one at a time. *This is really an important part of this technique.* As you look through those pivotal moments or processes in your life, some of them will feel good and some will be laced with bad feelings in varying degrees.

What is useful is to set aside 'unfinished business', and you can do that by identifying a time that was particularly uncomfortable. Let that be the title for a separate writing, and set your timer for five to ten minutes. Write about that uncomfortable time. Then jot down how it felt to release those feelings. You can pick any or all of your **Steppingstones** as a prompt for further writing. As we said earlier, it's a good idea to make them timed writings so you know when you are complete. This is part of Progoff's method for probing further into our inner depths.

James Pennebaker is a psychologist who has done research on self-expression. He has found that when people take time to write about difficult life experiences they display increased immune system functioning and decreased hypertension. We don't necessarily enjoy going back through difficult memories, but it can be very healing for us to do so as a way to release and heal them.

GO!

When you have finished that piece of writing, know that you can do the same with another of your **Steppingstones**. You can, as I said earlier, do your **Steppingstones** about different areas of your life but still use them as an opportunity to confront areas of your life that still have a 'charge' on them. **Steppingstones** is a wonderful technique to use when you want to create your own autobiography! Progoff also suggests using **Steppingstones** when you are doing a dialogue with another person, but we will cover that more in another project.

Did you like this technique? Are you aware of what kind of techniques
you like and which you don't like?
Pay attention as you continue on through the lessons.

Unsent Letters

This technique is just as it sounds. It may be one that you are already familiar with, but no matter, it is useful regardless of how many times in the past you may have tried it. I think this is the most common exercise that I give my clients in classes and in counseling, partly because everyone knows how to write a letter!

Unsent Letters allow you to express what you have to say without the person you are considering ever knowing what you are thinking or feeling. Now, it may happen, in some situations, that after you write you decide you *do* want to talk to them or write them another letter. That is fine. *NEVER*—repeat, *NEVER*—send an **Unsent Letter**. Private writing—journal writing—needs to be cleaned up before it is made public, *always*!

So, whom can you think of that you may want to send an **Unsent Letter** to? I used to think of **Unsent Letters** as always being negative or angry, but in fact it's possible that you may write some that are very loving and appreciative. Often we neglect to say thank you as frequently as we repress our angry words. Here are some examples of people you may want to send an **Unsent Letter** to:

- ➢ *A parent*
- ➢ *A partner*
- ➢ *A child*
- ➢ *A boss*

➢ *A co-worker*

➢ *A part of yourself*

➢ *God*

➢ *The President*

➢ *?*

Often, in my face-to-face classes, I ask people to write a letter of love and support to themselves—and that is what I am going to ask you to do now. Too often we get caught up in anger and resentment when what we really need is to be kind and loving to ourselves. This, I think, could be a useful exercise for *all* of us to do on a weekly basis.

So, again set your timer for as much time as you want to spend on this, and begin your letter of love and support to yourself.

GO!

About writing **Unsent Letters** to others: sometimes it takes writing a letter to a particular person more than one time in order to discharge the feelings that you have toward him or her. If so, just allow yourself to do it, over and over, if necessary. One of the big advantages of journal writing, as far as I'm concerned, is the ability to say what ever you want—repeatedly, if necessary. Sometimes our friends and family just don't have the patience to listen to our ramblings . . . but the journal is always there.

Perhaps you can set a time for yourself to write a letter of discharge to someone in the near future.

Creative Visualization

Creative Visualization is a technique used by many people to help them move toward achieving their life goals. It is a process that involves three major steps, which are: relaxation, visualization of a desired outcome, and repetition. Journaling supports this process and can be used repeatedly to help you achieve your desires. I recommend the books *You, the Healer,* by Jose Silva, and *Your Heart's Desire*, by Sonia Choquette, to help you gather more information and insight into this process.

For now, consider the following scenarios and what might fit best for you right now:

> ➤ See yourself as a success in some area of your life--parent, student, businessperson, etc.

> ➤ See yourself as healthy, vital and feeling glad to be alive.

> ➤ Imagine yourself interviewing a leader in your field of work, an expert on relationships, or your own inner healer. Find out what information they have to offer you.

> ➤ See yourself finishing an important task and being congratulated for a job well done.

Adapt one of these pictures to your life and think about what you would like to accentuate in your experiences. When you have decided, write that down on your page. Read through the following guided meditation to help you first to relax and then, perhaps, to make some discoveries about where you are and where you are going.

✦ Meditation ✦

Relax, allow your eyes to soften. Get comfortable in your chair. Take a deep breath . . . Now take another breath and as you do, feel yourself sinking more deeply into your chair, your arms feeling heavier and with less desire to move around. Let the tension lift away from you and notice how you can let go of everything, except the awareness of your own breathing . . . Imagine yourself transported to your favorite environment—a a beach, the forest, a stream, a meadow . . . Notice whether you are alone or if there is someone else there sharing your relaxation . . . wander around, enjoying the beauty and serenity of this special place. . . . Soon you come to a clearing where you find a gift or a message that relates to your life. You know that this is completely safe and you are able to receive this gift or message with great joy. . . .Give yourself time to take in the beauty, the gift or message and the joy of this special place . . . And when you are ready, take a deep breath, open your eyes and begin to write about relaxation and your special gift or message . . . or, draw a picture of your gift or message . . . allow yourself to open to your own wisdom and knowing..

✦

Creative Visualization is a kind of exercise that moves you beyond left-brain thinking into the imagery and vision of the right brain. Journal writing is, indeed, a whole-brain process, allowing you to operate in the linear, logical and verbal left brain while also allowing you to tap into the emotional, imaginative and visionary capabilities of the right brain. Journaling allows the critic that is so much a part of the left-brain to step aside and take a break. When that happens, the *'magic'* of our greater selves is able to open and offer us deeper and more meaningful guidance.

There are many different ways that you can use the power of **Creative Visualization**. You may simply want to use the 'sanctuary' you found in the first part of the above exercise to get you to a place of peace and relaxation. From there, you can ask all kinds of questions of your inner knowing. The more you do this kind of exercise and get yourself into a relaxed state, the more success you will have with **Creative Visualization.**

You have now completed the second class in the Basic Journaling series.
Please take some time to make notes about
what you liked and what you didn't like. Between this class
and the next, practice all eight approaches that have been covered so far.
Make note of how your journaling has changed.

Basic Journaling –
Lesson Three of Four

I hope that by now you are enjoying the increased repertoire you have for your journaling practice. And I think the word 'practice' does offer another view of journal writing---that it is a practice, like meditation, yoga, or prayer. And journaling, as you may have discovered by now, can, indeed, take you into places of great peace, knowing and joy. For me, having access to a variety of techniques that I can put together in various combinations, allows me to move more deeply into my life, my goals and my depths.

In this class we will again cover four different kinds of techniques. They are: **Special Moments, Lists, Dialogue** and **Alphapoems**. All will present you with yet another way to express your views, wishes and creative endeavors.

Before we move into the first technique, I want to share a few of my favorite quotes with you about the medium of journaling. There are many fine books on the subject—many more than I would have believed when I began my studies in this field.

Tristine Rainer is the author of **The New Diary**, a very detailed history of the journal or diary. She uses the terms interchangeably. She says, "The diary is the only form of writing that encourages total freedom of expression. Because of its very private nature, it has remained immune to any formal rules of content, structure, or style. As a result, the diary can come closest to reproducing how people really think and how consciousness evolves."

In as much as authenticity is one of my values, I can see, based on this quote, why journaling has been so meaningful to me. It *does* offer us a mirror of ourselves! She goes on to say, "Using the diary effectively depends only upon the degree to which you trust your intuition and your process. The very act of sitting down with the diary signifies a readiness to commune with the self; and the very act of writing may place you inside the mystery of self-healing and self-recreation, no matter what is written or how it is expressed."

I think this is a very important concept to be aware of—and it provides good reason for you to take some time to congratulate yourself for having the willingness to dig in and write about yourself. This is not easy.

Many people push journals away because to write things down is too scary. As you see yourself in what you have written you are forced to own, to really see, what has gone on in your life. It may lead you to confront various conflicts or inconsistencies in your life. So, while we may discover wonderful wisdom within, we may also have to confront some of our inner demons, as well. The journal provides a space for dealing with all of our concerns, one step at a time.

We could say, *"Journaling is Not For Sissies!"*

I promise you that Tristine's book is full of quotable passages and invite you to explore further. (Quotes can also become a wonderful way to get started in your journaling, using one as a prompt for further writing. Try Googling "quotes" to see what shows up!)

Special Moments

Let's move ahead now and explore another technique, one called **Special Moments**. This, like **Favorite People**, is a descriptive exercise. It offers you the opportunity to create verbal photographs of those special moments in your life. We all have these memories, whether we tend to be visual, kinesthetic or auditory, and we save our precious—and sometimes traumatic—experiences within our very cells. To tap into these memories we need only relax into a guided meditation.

Before you settle into the guided meditation that follows, you may want to think about (or make a short list) of some events that bring up immediate pictures in your mind's eye. Then I recommend that you make a decision—an agreement with yourself—about *what kind of experience you choose to have.* Do you want to move into an area that will bring you new growth and awareness but may be uncomfortable, or do you want to go to a time of joyful remembrance and savor the beauty of a particular time? I offer this suggestion because the first time I did it I went for growth—-and I found myself in a traumatic time in my life. It was useful, I think, in helping me to release the trauma, but it was a surprise in such an 'innocent' exercise. Just remember that we always have choices about how we want to proceed. It is very important to be respectful of our needs in any given moment.

You might be surprised at how much of a given situation you are able to recall. When you allow yourself to be still and go into a gentle meditation, the vividness of your memory can be astounding. When you are there, imagine yourself to be a reporter describing the who, what, where, why and how of the time while also looking for the mood, emotion, energy and bodily sensations you experience as you relive this time. Your descriptive vocabulary will simply emerge for you as you put yourself back in the scene.

Read quietly to yourself or have someone read to you:

✦ Meditation ✦

Allow yourself, now, to get very comfortable in your chair, sitting back, letting go of 'shoulds' and 'have-tos' for the next few minutes. You are free, for now, and need only focus on your breath in each moment. Notice your breathing as you settle in more deeply. Release any tension that stands out for you and enjoy the openness of this moment.

As you sit there comfortably, allow yourself to imagine your mind as a window blind that has just been pulled down. You see only the blankness of it and all else that you have been aware of has been temporarily erased.

You may now invite events from your life to pass by on that window blind, becoming like a movie screen of your life. Let events pass by one by one just observing but not yet holding on to any one.

As you see these images pass by in your mind's eye, you remember that you have chosen a particular kind of memory that you want to explore further. You begin to focus in on just one such memory and see, hear, feel and know this scene more and more clearly. You feel yourself there, no longer looking at a screen but now feeling yourself present in that scene.

Let your awareness roam as you scan this time and place from your life. Drink in the details. Pick up on colors, sounds, smells, energy, emotions going on around and in you. Your descriptors will pop up as you re-experience this very special moment. Your inner feelings will be exaggerated as you allow yourself to be drenched in the completeness of this time. Stay there, immersing yourself in your own personal history as long as you like.

When you are ready, bring those back with you to the place you are sitting. Gently breathe, and pick up your pen. Then begin to flow with the remembrance of your special moment. Allow about 10 minutes for this writing.

✦

You may want to take a break at this time, or you may want to proceed. Jot down what you liked and didn't like about the previous technique. Were there surprises for you? Can you think of different kinds of situations in which you would want to use this technique? What other techniques might you combine with this one that would take you to a deeper place? Now that you have more techniques available to you, you will begin to get a sense of how you can combine them for greater inner knowing.

The next technique that we will explore is a simple one, one that you have already done countless times in your life but may not have thought of as a journal writing technique. It is:

Lists

Lists help us by: clearing the clutter out of our minds, helping us to sort out various steps of a given task, clarifying time requirements, brainstorming ideas, and exploring unconscious desires. Surprised that so much can come from a **list**?

We all do **Short Lists**---those daily chores we want to finish *today*, like: who needs a card sent to them, whom to invite to your party, and what to serve at your party. This kind of **Short List** saves us much energy by having our concerns written down and not needing to have everything on the 'hard-drive' of our brains. As I get older I need **Lists** more and more.

Longer Lists can help you dig a little deeper. They can be used for brainstorming about a particular topic such as,

➢ *The hopes you have for your life*

➢ *The qualities you desire in your friends*

➢ *Activities you want to add to your schedule to increase your fun*

➢ *People who inspire you*

➢ *Goals you feel good about having met*

When you do these **Longer Lists**, you must write as quickly as you can, write down everything, not censoring any thought, and you can repeat ideas as often as you want. I use this technique when I brainstorm ideas for a speech, titles for my workshops, or when I'm thinking about other ways to use journaling!

For our purposes now, we will do **Really Long Lists—lists to 100!** This kind of list making not only allows you to brainstorm a particular theme but also dredges up ideas from your unconscious. As in the above exercise, you number each item, write quickly, and repeat as often as you like. You are not to censor any ideas and are not to worry about making sense.

When you have finished your list to 100 you will be able to count how often you repeated a particular idea—which can give you a register of intensity of interest as well as a percentage of your 100 ideas! For instance, if you make a list of stressors in your life, you may find that you mentioned one kind of stress 24 times—which would be 24% of all your stressors. You will also find that you come up with more ideas from your unconscious in the last third of your list. That's the main advantage to a **Really Long List**—we can pull up more information from our hidden selves.

Choose from the following list, or create your own topic for your list to 100:

➢ *100 things that make me happy*

➢ *100 feelings I have about money*

➢ *100 things I like about my work*

➢ *100 obstacles that keep me from complete success*

➢ *100 things I feel sad about.*

GO!

So, now that you are finished with your **List,** how do you feel? Where did it take you? Once again, can you see how this could be combined with another technique to take you to a deeper place? Progoff often combined small lists with many of his techniques as a way of creating a gentle progression. As a matter of fact, our next technique could utilize a **Short List** to help set it up. The next technique is:

Dialogue

This is a very powerful and exciting technique that can also be used in a variety of ways. Consider who and what you dialogue with in your life today. That is a place to start. With whom would you like to have a 'practice' conversation? Anyone with whom you have unfinished business? This technique is similar to the **Unsent Letter** but in this case allows the other person to respond. It can be very revealing!

Besides people, you may find it useful to **Dialogue** with parts of yourself, like that stomach that keeps 'talking' to you, or your heart that feels broken. Just give those parts of you a voice and discover new perspectives. **Dialogue**s can be held with people wiser than you, on subjects like money or work, and even with people who have died or are not yet born.

Dialogues are very revealing and very dynamic. You may be surprised by what you know.

Begin by making a **Short List** of people who are or have been important to you. Once you have written those names down, look for one with whom you have special energy or excitement. If you want to do this exercise as Progoff would have presented it, you can do **Steppingstones** for this other person before you begin your **Dialogue**. If not, just begin your **Dialogue** as though you were writing a script. Who will begin? Start with wherever you experience the most energy/excitement and just go from there. See what transpires.

For those who would like some help in 'feeling into'" the other side of the **Dialogue**, you can do **Steppingstones** for that person, as I mentioned in introducing **Steppingstones**. If, for instance, I wanted to do a **Dialogue** with a friend with whom I am estranged, I could begin their **Steppingstones** with "I was born . . .." Additional steps would come either from what I know about the person or from what I imagine. The point is to get into their skin, to open awareness about them, and to prepare to be able to make some guesses as to how they may participate in a **Dialogue**. I hope you will try this to see the added power it can provide to your **Dialogue**.

If you would rather not **Dialogue** with a person, then try something else—like work, money, values, health or energy as partners in your **Dialogue**. I have had wonderful **Dialogue**s with money! Once your topic is clear, think about approximately how much time you want to spend, then . . .

GO!

You may have more processing to do after this exercise. Read over your **Dialogue** and consider what has come up. Do you need more time to process? Are there other techniques that might help you clarify or complete this experience? Can you get a sense of how powerful this **Dialogue** technique is? Realize, at the same time, that the power has come from *you*. This technique is a rich and empowering way for you to experience more of yourself.

The last technique in this section is one of my favorites. It is one that can be used after a heavy experience, like what may have just come up for you in **Dialogue** or as an icebreaker, at the beginning of a class or retreat time.

Alphapoem

Alphapoems are created by writing the alphabet vertically down the side of your page. You will then use each letter as the first letter of each word in each line of your poem. Now, this might sound simplistic---I thought so when I first did it--but it can bring up amazing things! Before you begin an **Alphapoem**, it's best to consider a topic or theme for your poem. You could, for instance, write about *power* and how you experience it more fully after your writing experiences. What issues have come up as you have done the other techniques? Do you have a strong emotional feeling going on for you right now? This can be a rich well from which to draw. When all else fails, do your **Alphapoem** on Gratitude. We never take enough time to acknowledge all we have to be grateful for! Here's another kind of **Alphapoem**, one that came from one of my classes. It uses just the word that is being described---and could as easily be the name of a person.

Alphapoem on "POWERFUL"

P resent and powerful, here and now, I
O wn my
W isdom,
E ver mindful of others' needs, yet honoring my own,
R esponding to others and self
F ully,
U nendingly,
L ovingly.

- Anne Lackey, August 2003

Anne is a friend and a frequent participant in my Online Journal Classes, so with her permission I am happy to share that piece to help you see how they can be done. It's easiest to write quickly, not thinking too hard, simply letting the letters guide you. Now, do your own, using the whole alphabet—on your chosen topic!

GO!

Aren't you surprised at what you came up with? The letters seem to guide us along, forcing us to choose words we wouldn't perhaps come up with on our own. It allows unconscious thoughts and feelings to sneak out onto the page. Make note of your reactions while doing this technique and feel free to share those thoughts with me by email.

Now, for some review of the Project. What stands out? How did you feel about the flow from one exercise to another? This is something you will think about more and more as you begin putting exercises together. Be aware of which techniques you enjoyed and which you didn't and how you think you could use them in the future. Experiment with them further so you really get a feel for them. Do the entire Project over again. You will find your experience different each time!

> *Okay, this is the end of the third lesson. Practice these techniques several times before we move on to the next lesson. It will help you connect with them and keep your journaling habit going.*

Basic Journaling –
Lesson Four of Four

Here you are, ready to embark on the fourth lesson in **Basic Journaling**. I hope you are finding as useful as you expected— or even more so. When you finish this installment you will have practiced sixteen different kinds of journal writing techniques. This variety of techniques will allow you to choose different approaches for different situations you find yourself in. As you combine techniques or do them repetitively, you will find yourself reaching greater and greater depth. What you have learned in this series of lessons is much like learning about different ingredients used in baking. You can put them together in an infinite number of ways to make new delectable treats!

We will cover four more techniques in this lesson: **Collections, Freewriting, Inner Wisdom,** and **Perspectives**.

Another of the books that I particularly like about the journal writing process is one by G. Lynn Nelson, a professor at Arizona State University. His book is called ***Writing and Being***, and I highly recommend it. I will share with you some tidbits from this valuable book. He talks in depth about the importance of writing from one's heart and not just 'doing it right,' as so many of us were taught in school. He explains that our educational system taught most of us to write properly—but when we did that at a young age, we left out our heart, saying:

> *"The simple act of starting with the heart," he says, "can transform both our writing and our being. As we take back our feelings, value and validate them, acknowledge and explore them, we experience a new creativity and power in our words and a new vitality in our lives."*

He later says,

> *"No one said anything about where the "stuff" to write about came from. No one told me the place to start was within myself or suggested*

that writing was, in itself, a way to discover things about myself and the world. I was taught to write when I had something (public) to say, so I seldom wrote. Now, I write in my journal to find out what I have to say—so I am forever writing."

I could offer many more of his quotes but will end with this one:

"The great power of journal writing is that it enables us, without our having to know or understand consciously how it works, to begin living our lives actively rather than reactively. As we work in our journals, we make choices we could not make before, because we could not see, because we were trapped in the small vision of that small identity. We live more creatively and begin to become the artists of our own lives."

I hope these few brief extracts will spur you toward reading his whole book, which is full of wisdom and profundity. You will be moved by it.

You can see that I have collected some quotes of people I respect. It is a kind of **Collection**--which is the technique we will talk about first in this lesson. When I was young I loved to collect things: seashells, colored glass washed up on the beach, porcelain dogs, silver spoons----can you relate?

Collections

Your journal—or a journal—can be used to hold special treasures and special **Collections**, too. Use your imagination and your special interests to help you decide what kind of **Collections** to maintain. This is a childlike activity that many adults will find to be fun, fanciful, touching, individual and satisfying. Of course, *Memory Books*, that are so popular now, are one version of special collections.

This is a creative technique that takes you away from writing per se. You may want to keep a notebook that is *just* for this special **Collection**. I have a few suggestions that might help spur your imagination. You could collect:

➢ *Favorite quotes (could even be your own!)*
➢ *Inventions (things you think would improve your life)*
➢ *Happy moments (like "happygrams" our kids got in school—to our selves)*
➢ *Special gifts*
➢ *A wish list*

> ➢ *Endings to "When I grow up I want to be…"*
> ➢ *Compliments*
> ➢ *Ideas for improving the world*

You get the picture.

Whatever theme you pick, you might want to decorate your journal in a special way. Take some time to create a separate journal—or just decorate the one you are using currently. Try pictures, words from magazines, colored paper, stickers—whatever makes you feel good. Allow yourself time to be young at heart and creative!

You may want to do a **Five Minute Sprint** or a **Cluster** about what kinds of **Collections** you would like to maintain! What does this kind of creative exercise bring up for you? Of course, as you add things to your **Collection**, be sure to take time to *write* about how you feel about it.

Consider, too, creating a special space in your daily planner. Create a section where you can keep special ideas, feelings, 'happenings'. Your imagination will be nourished by this return to a youthful approach to Personal Treasures! I know you will have many more ideas about the kinds of **Collections** you want to create.

We will move on now, and describe the next technique. It is referred to as:

Freewriting

You will find references to this technique by Tristine Rainer, Kathleen Adams, Christina Baldwin and Julia Cameron. *It is, quite simply, the kind of stream-of-consciousness writing that many people think of as journal writing.*

Freewriting is a technique in which we have little concern with punctuation, grammar or complete sentences. As I said, many people view this as *"the way to do journal writing"*—and it is certainly one way to do it.

Let me give you a brief example of some I did this morning:

"Great morning – beautiful. Bright sunshine. Temperature rising. Off for walk with the dog. Stopping for meditation . . . interrupted by warning bark of the dog. Entered the quiet, long remembered darkness of unending love and deep care. Sitting there, releasing reluctantly so as to function on this plane. Remembered peace amidst great pain. Knowing. Giving up the struggle. Releasing. Trusting. Moving beyond words. Peace. Peace. Seeing the crack into eternity

and just being there. Just being. My path. Gets clearer . . . and less wordy."

The word processor would not let some of those words not be capitalized but I think you can get the idea. It was time between worlds, so to speak, where I was able to just jot down the flow rather than worrying about the form or trying to make sense.

Though it seems on the surface that this is a very simple kind of writing, it is actually the most difficult. This kind of free form can be very intimidating to a beginner. It requires focus and personal centering, which is not always something we have access to. It can be difficult and discouraging to not only begin but to sustain the movement. It is why I encourage you to begin with the **Five Minute Sprint** about a particular question—giving you boundaries and focus.

Freewriting is best done when you are in a very stable, centered place (or after you have done some preliminary sprints). It is abstract and uncontained and unbounded. I have put it in this last class because you now have enough experience to discern the feelings you have as you do this technique.

To set yourself up for some **Freewriting** you may want to imagine yourself out of doors, sitting by a stream. You begin to watch the stream flow past you and before long feel yourself entering into the flow. You move with the stream and allow yourself to bump along, being carried from one awareness to another.

Allow yourself to **Freewrite** for as long as you desire. There are no constraints on **Freewriting**.

Go!

What was your experience of **Freewriting**? Can you see how sometimes this will feel perfect for you and at other times may make you uncomfortable? Julia Cameron, who wrote **The Artist's Way**, suggests to her readers that they do "Morning Pages." What she means by this is that a person should write three pages each morning. Every morning. This is **Freewriting**. By doing it first thing in the morning, she believes, we learn to get around our inner critic and into our right-brain creativity. You may want to give it a try, so get her book. It's another good one! And **Freewriting** is a powerful exercise.

The next technique is another one of my favorites. Actually, it is the one technique that I have used most for my own personal growth. I have done this particular exercise—with my own variations—for well over twenty years. The technique is called:

Inner Wisdom

This technique helps you to access your inner knowing, your intuition, a guardian angel, a guide—or just God. You will use whatever term fits best into your own belief system. The idea comes from the belief that we are all connected to much greater wisdom and awareness than we can really imagine. If we take the time, on a regular basis, to slow down, ask our questions, and listen for the answers, we can be guided in a very powerful way throughout our lives.

By listening and nurturing our inner knowing, we are able to learn to *trust* ourselves. As we learn to trust this knowing, we can be better prepared to maintain balance in a world that, at least in the United States, is very externally oriented.

Your **Inner Wisdom** will help you to stop and listen. Use it honorably. Take your serious concerns to this part of yourself. Enter your sacred space with love and respect—and expect to receive answers to your questions in a variety of forms.

To begin, identify a question or area of concern that you may have and write it down. Then put your pen down and read or have the following read to you:

✦ Meditation ✦

As you sit in your quiet and special place, allow yourself to take a gentle and nourishing breath. As you exhale allow yourself to imagine releasing all inhibition about listening. Give yourself the freedom to enter into your own sacred space. Each time that you return it will feel warmer, richer and more nurturing.

Imagine now that you are going on an inner journey. A journey to your sacred space, a place that holds your connection to all wisdom, all knowing, all love. You move to this space at your own pace and feel its peace and beauty and you get closer to it. You know when you enter into this special center and feel your question and concerns being lightened just knowing that there is guidance within reach.

As you look around you know why this is your sacred space. It contains just those aspects from your life that are important to you. It may resemble a scene from nature, a temple, a church or you may be in the company of your mentor. Give yourself time to appreciate and enjoy this aspect of perfection that you hold within you.

> *When you feel at ease, ask the question that you have brought with you. Expect your answer to come in words, symbols, gestures, pictures, visions—in any of many different forms. Listen to that wisdom that you access by asking your question. Take in the response given to you in whatever form it appears. Let it fill and enliven you. When you feel you have received all that you need for now, bring yourself back to your pen, your paper and begin to write your experience of your inner wisdom.*

✦

Well, how do you feel? Could be a little spacey or as though you are floating. This technique asks you to let go of your left-brain leanings and tap into your more creative right brain. It is not a good exercise to use if you are feeling stressed or anxious. This exercise is best done when you are feeling in a very good, stable place. I often use this exercise to close a group because it creates its own kind of closure. You want to be careful about jumping into other activities right after doing this. Allow yourself to savor the feelings of relaxation and letting go.

I hope that you will find this technique as useful in your life as I have.

So, here we are at our last technique! When you master this you will have the complete repertoire of journaling techniques.

Perspectives

Perspectives is a technique that allows you to use your imagination to put your into the life of another person, to 'live' in a different place, or to imagine yourself transported into a different time!

> ➢ Become your favorite historical figure! What would Benjamin Franklin have to say about our government today? Or what would a pioneer woman say about today's modern conveniences? Pursue a time in history, or imagine a futuristic world filled with people from different planets. Let this stretch your imagination and exercise your descriptive language!

> ➢ Imagine yourself living in a different place--someplace totally different from where you now live. Thinking about moving? Let yourself imagine many different settings. Write down your response to each environment—and let it ease your decision.

➢ My personal favorite use of this technique is to imagine myself either forward or backward in time. You can write a journal entry for one year from today and imagine and the changes that have come to pass in your life. This can be particularly useful to assist you in goal setting. Figure out where you would like to be and work backwards!

Okay, now it's time to do it! My suggestion is that you imagine yourself one year from now. What are you working on now that you would like to see concluded by then? What surprises might come? Who will the people be in your life? What will your job, house, or car be like? Play with this a little. Don't get too stuck in trying to be *right on.* Just let your intuition and imagination work together to paint you a picture of the life you hope you are creating!

Picture your calendar. Whatever day it is today, add a year, and start your journal entry, describing the year just past.

GO!

Allow as much time as you desire.

This is one that will be fun to return to—to check out the accuracy of what you imagined!

I'd like to ask you now to take a few days to think about—and perhaps even write about—the lessons you have completed. What did you learn? What were some meaningful experiences? Do you feel that your journal writing will be more useful, focused, deep, what? How has this helped you toward developing your journal writing . . . and ultimately toward creating a more peaceful relationship with yourself?

I honor you. Namaste.

This is the end of our four-lesson Course in Basic Journaling. Continue to practice these techniques from this day forward. Such practice will help you connect with yourself and your world, and the magic of journaling will help to make your journaling more and more productive as time passes!

A Further Introduction

Now that you have reviewed the basics of journal writing, you are ready to fully enter into the sessions that follow. Over time, I have come to believe that these techniques might better be called "**Therapeutic Writing**," an enhanced perspective on journaling. As you proceed, you will see why this label seems to work, and I think you will agree.

There are twelve different **"Projects"** for you to enjoy, each giving you four different writing sessions. You can go through these projects in order, or you may choose to jump around according to your interests.

Create a Group?

One way to enjoy these sessions even more is to do them within a group. I have become a great believer in group journaling because it seems to deepen the experience for each person involved in a way that is richer and more profound than when journaling alone. You will see occasional suggestions for sharing within your group as you move through these projects. If you are working through the exercises on your own, just ignore those remarks (and know you could repeat the exercises again and again, alone or in a group, always with the fresh perspective of that time in your life).

You may already have a group of friends who would be interested in joining with you to create a group, or you might explore your clubs and churches to search for additional members. Four or five folks seems to be a nice number for a living room group. Allow about two hours per session.

If you do create a small group, here are just a few guidelines to follow to help everyone feel safe and secure.

It is important that **no one** be **required** to read from their journal—they may, if they choose, but must never be made to read something they are not ready to share. Additionally, if someone does read something they have written, be sure to be respectful, to listen with attention, but not to criticize or make suggestions--- or to offer advice.

Keeping what is shared in the group confidential adds another level of safety to those present and helps to provide a setting where deeper feelings can be expressed. Friendships can deepen in a kindness-dominated group of this type. I hope you will consider which of your friends would enjoy this gentle and creative group experience with you.

You will know I am making a suggestion for group sharing when you see this symbol:

◆ *So let this be a guide for questions and sharing in the group—adding others as you see fit!*

Whether in a group or on your own, there is much ahead to explore—and *so much more magic to find within!* Enjoy your exploration!

Finding the Jewels
As You Clear Away the Clutter

We all have so much *stuff* in our western culture! Besides the huge amounts of physical *things*, we also have the emotional *stuff* that clutters our minds and hearts and keeps many of us whirring into the night. My suggestion for you in this project is to take a look at, and perhaps let go of the clutter, so you can see more clearly your strengths—the jewels in and of your life. You may find that the inner clutter has more of an impact on your physical experience, and vice-versa, than you realized.

Remember the most basic tenet of journaling: *there is no right way to do it* except as it fits for you. Therefore, there are no rules per se, though there are suggestions that can make your journaling more effective. I don't think it hurts to review guidelines (stated just a little differently than earlier).

- One is: always date your entries so you can understand context if you want to go back and read them later.
- Another is: take a little time to *breathe and relax* before you begin, shaking off some of the day's stress.
- Yet another: write as you would speak or as you think, not worrying about grammar, spelling or punctuation.
- Very important: guard your privacy—if you are worried that someone else will read your writing you will not be totally honest with yourself, and as a result you'll miss some of your "magic."

- Finally—and at least as important as all of the above: **have fun** with your journal.

Session 1

I always start by asking people to write for up to five minutes about whatever is on their minds. A good question to ask yourself is: "What have I been keeping myself from saying today? Or, "What is it I need to get out of the way so I can be fully present? Or, you may just want to respond to the question, "What's going on?" This allows you to shift your attention from what is going on *outside* of you to what is going on *inside* of you. This attention is part of what we need in today's world, and it's where our hidden power and other treasures lie—once we let go of some of the *junk* we've collected.

We'll start each session with this exercise, which I have labeled as the **Five Minute Sprint**. I learned it from Kathleen Adams of *Journal to the Self*, and it is the most practical of all journal-writing techniques—like this:

    I.   Take a deep breath, pick up your pen, notice the time . . . and begin to write, with no agenda. Take five minutes to "warm up" and get yourself going by responding to one of the suggested questions or simply expressing how you feel.

When your five minutes are up, take a moment to reflect on your experience. How do you feel now as compared to how you felt as you began? Do you feel the 'shift' that happens as you take time for yourself? Write a sentence about that, if you choose.

Hopefully, you have your **JournalCards** and can get them out to help you deepen your inner focus. As you shuffle the cards, think about just what you need to be reminded of today. This is also a part of the routine within these sessions. As you move from one exercise to another, you move into deeper parts of yourself. The **Five Minute Sprint** gets you started, and the **JournalCards** help you gain new focus.

    II.   Now, draw your first card. As you read it over, let it trigger ideas, feelings and even additional questions. You may want to draw one more card, to help you focus even more on the aspect of your life that is now in your awareness.

As you read your card, noting the word, the picture, and the questions, begin to write about what has been "stirred up" for you. Let the card simply remind you of your deeper questions and wider vision. No need to try to answer all the questions, just go with the parts that speak to you now.

As you work through these exercises you may want to make a habit of underlining important thoughts or writing questions or comments in the margins of your journal. Remember that this is YOUR space, to do with as you choose. Think about how you want to track ideas that you may want to write about at another time.

III. The last piece we will do in this session is to take a meditative tour of your house. So often the comparison is made between our home and our being. So how far does this analogy work for you? Allow yourself some time to breathe gently and read slowly this little meditation. See what images arise for you as you write this description. Later you can re-read it and see if the description also fits for you and your personality.

✦ Meditation ✦

Take a gentle breath, and allow yourself to breathe it in deeply, taking it in and then releasing it ever so smoothly.
Do this several times, allowing yourself to release tension and distractions from the day . . .
We are going to go on an imaginative journey . . .
You are going to let go of your physical being for now . . .
and imagine that you are about to walk into your own home as if for the first time.
Don't look around now if you are at home, but just go with your inner image.
Note how you feel as you drive up to your house, get out of the car and walk to the front entrance.
See with fresh eyes as you walk to your house.
Be observant. You will be able to report your observations when you are ready to write . . .
As you touch the doorknob, turn it . . .
and walk in the front door,
what happens?
How do you feel?
What do you see?
What do you perceive about the energy of this space?
Scan the room for objects, colors, smells that stand out.

Walk around the room and see more, more of what is in this entry and central living area . . .
When you are ready, move toward the bedroom and continue your exploration . . .
Breathe. . .
Pay attention to all of your senses, as your attention takes you from one focus to another. . .
and then another. . .
And now you move to the bathroom.
As you enter you open a drawer to see what has been put there.
What do the contents of the drawer tell you about the people who live here?
Take another deep breath. . .
and sense the emotions that live here.
Look around once again, taking a mental inventory of what you see and how you feel. . . . Next, take yourself to the kitchen, looking in the refrigerator, opening drawers and just snooping— as though you are seeing the house for the first time . . .

What do you make of this place?
Who do you think lives here?
What assumptions do you make about this house based on what you've seen?
Is there much clutter here?
Does it need more care?
Or is it well cared for and peaceful?
Take another deep breath as you ready yourself to pick up your pen and write.

✦

Explore your ideas about this house you have just visited. Write down the first impressions you had that popped into your awareness as you 'walked' through your house. Write a full description of what you encountered and how you felt as you moved from room to room.

When you are done take some time to write about how your description of the house might fit for *you* and for your physical and emotional self? Explore these ideas as long as you desire.

◆ *If you are working on this within a group, you might all take some time to share parts of your "hits" that arise as you explore the house in comparison to your physical self. Other things you may want to share are general discoveries in doing journaling this way rather than just sitting and free-writing (meaning writing as a stream of consciousness without specific guidance).*

How did the ***JournalCards*** fit? Whether you're doing these exercises on your own or in a group, take a few minutes to describe your experience. What did you think of having a **Five Minute Sprint** to get you started? And what about the cards? Were you surprised at what came up after reading them?

Session 2

You are ready now to begin another session of this project about clutter vs. clarity. The format is the same as Session 1, beginning with the **Five Minute Sprint**, then ***JournalCards***, and then some additional exercises. Each time you start a new session you may find it meaningful to review what you wrote in the previous session.

I.   Again, start with a general clearing by writing for five minutes. Start with a question as simple as "What is happening?" and just get your pen moving. Use this time to dump feelings that you've been holding onto that keep you from being fully available right now. Just let them go as you write.

II.   Now that you are 'warmed up,' take a breath and pick a ***JournalCard***. Give yourself time to see how it might stir you up and help you to consider some aspect of your life. Choose another if you want, to enhance and deepen your awareness. Write again for about five to ten minutes about your reactions to the cards and how they fit for your life today.

Are you realizing more of your inner wealth and magic as you move from the surface of your life into deeper and more thoughtful areas? As you consider more about the clutter vs. the jewels within your life, what comes to mind as the obstacles that keep you from the jewels? How do you lose track of your inner essence, your inner power and beauty?

III.   Make a **List** of all the clutter you have in your life, from distracting thoughts to stacks of papers to household chores. Don't censor! Write it all down. When you create a list, number as you go, write quickly, it's okay to repeat, and make your list as long as you can—at least to 25 and longer if you can.

The following exercise will help you to see how much further you can still go as you reach deeper and deeper within and move closer and closer to the magic that is you. This technique is called a **"Series of Three"** and was taught to me by Kathleen Adams, author of ***Journal to the Self,*** a name you should be feeling very familiar with by now. You will begin this three-part exercise with another **Five Minute Sprint**. In order to pick a fitting title for this exercise you need to consider what you've learned about your self and clutter so far. Do you see how you block yourself from your gifts and talents—your jewels?

The title I would suggest to you is **"How clutter keeps me from my true self."** Feel free to rework the wording to make it ring true for you. The point is to address how clutter, in some form, keeps you from expressing your essential self.

IV. Once you have gotten clear about your title, begin a **Five Minute Sprint** on that topic. When you are through, read through it and underline words and phrases that hit you as key or meaningful, or push you forward in some way.

V. Then, pick one of those phrases as the title for your next **Five Minute Sprint** and *go*. Write again for five minutes. When you're done, again underline significant words and phrases and again pick the one that has the most interest for you as the title for your third **Five Minute Sprint**. This kind of series will help you to move more deeply into yourself and your deeper consciousness, and you may find yourself surprised at what comes out.

Read over what you have written. Give yourself a few minutes to write about your reaction to your **Series of Three**.

◆*And again, this is often good material to share with your larger group if you are involved in one. By now you are hopefully feeling more comfortable with the whole process and may find you have much to share.*

Session 3

Going through this process in each session helps you in several ways. For one thing, it does help you to begin where you are---which is always where we must begin but sometimes confuse ourselves thinking we should be more advanced. It is a practice of acceptance, of being present and aware of what is going on at the surface of our lives. As we write for those initial five minutes we make the shift from outer focus to inner awareness.

    I.   Take a deep breath as you pick up your pen and open your journal. Time yourself for five minutes to help you make the shift, become more aware of yourself, and get your pen moving on the page. Remember not to judge what you write…but simply to let this get you rolling.

    II.   Pick *JournalCards* again. As you choose cards this time, again take a deep breath. Think about your life, the clutter that invades it, and the jewels that you hold within. As you draw *JournalCards*, you might just ask for some guidance in this regard. What do your cards hint at as a way for you to improve your quality of life?

◆ *If you are doing these exercises in a group I encourage you all to take a turn at talking a little about the cards you've drawn, and as much or as little as you want to say about how they fit for your life—and for dipping into more of your "jewels".*

You've gathered more data about yourself now, the clutter and distractions you have around you, and how they may keep you from your riches within. Let's take this now one step further:

    III.   Make a **List** . . . of all the kinds of clutter and distractions that you want to release. Use your list from last session to help you focus on those things you are really ready now, to let go of. Write, "I release …" and complete that as many times as you can. (If you want to add an extra step, you could write these on a separate piece of paper and then burn them to add to your symbolic release.)

    IV.   Write a prayer to whatever Higher Power you believe in, asking for help and guidance as you release these obstacles from your life. Ask, too, for clarity about your gifts and talents that they will show themselves to you more clearly.

Take a deep breath now, appreciating the hard work you are doing and enjoying the new awarenesses that you have!

Session 4

Welcome back for our last session in this project. I hope you are enjoying this experience and feeling some satisfaction about what you have uncovered about yourself in the process.

I.   Begin again, as with other sessions, writing about whatever strikes you as important in this moment, just letting your pen—and hand—carry you to whatever thoughts or feelings that need to be released. Continue to experiment with just letting it flow for about five minutes.

II.   Now you can draw your ***JournalCard*** and see what appears before you. How does it relate to you, your life and the work you have been doing so far? If you choose, you can pull another card to deepen or expand your perception of what is going on now in your life. Experiment, if you want, with even one more card. Does it fit? Begin to write and see how the cards move you toward more clarity as you write. *Give yourself five to ten minutes for this writing.*

◆ *Remember that if you are working in a group you may again want to share your* ***JournalCards*** *and talk about how they assist you in your discovery process.*

III.   **Guided Meditation**. Here we go with another guided meditation—and you can go to the same house you went to in the first meditation, or any house you desire. Breathe gently, giving yourself plenty of uninterrupted time to settle in for your journey.

✦ Meditation ✦

Give yourself time, now to just breathe gently, to release any tensions or frustrations from your day . . . Breathe again, knowing you are nourishing your own very special body and soul. . . . As you breathe, feel the peace of knowing that you have done good work as you have metaphorically "cleaned house" . . . You are able to feel that sense of work well done, and sink more deeply into yourself . . .

Now you find yourself once again in front of a house . . . Look carefully at the structure of this place as you walk in and explore from room to room. Know that this is an extremely SAFE place, a place where peace and comfort resonate all around . . . As you feel the safety embracing you, go down the next hallway you see . . . There may be a short hall and then a longer hall . . . As you walk down each hallway you notice that the doors are all marked with different aspects of YOU, such as parent self, child self, worker bee, rest and relaxing self, and playful self—-and of course your doors will be marked especially for you . . . All these doors are unlocked . . . well, most of them are. There are a few, titled or not, that are locked up tight. And there is one of those in particular that . . . all of a sudden OPENS UP!!! It is a special room full of aspects of you that you are only now uncovering. The feelings are easily discernable as you enter the room and absorb the surroundings . . . There is nothing you need do here, but soak it up, and feel parts of yourself opening, opening . . . Stay with the experience . . . Feel the joy of knowing the magic you carry that has just become more available to you . . .

As you prepare to leave this beautiful house, look again at the doorways that are open, and even those that are closed, knowing that your loving spirit can help you open the rest when the time is right. As you leave notice the feelings you have about not only this special house, but also the very special you as well.

Begin now to prepare to return to your awareness of what is going on around you, feeling yourself in your chair and preparing to bring your new awareness into your lighted room. And slowly wiggle your toes and fingers, pick up your pen and begin to describe this wonderful house with many, many doorways.

✦

Take as much time as you need to write about this adventure. Notice especially your feelings about yourself and your house. Give yourself permission to describe and express all that has come up for you.

  IV. We need to plug in our journaling discoveries in our day-to-day lives, and not just leave them sitting in our journals. With that in mind, consider what specific *Action Steps*—which I like to call *Baby Steps*—could you create for yourself right now based on what you have learned in your journal writing exercises? Write them down, put them into your planner, or tell a friend about your *Action Steps* so you will be sure to follow through.

◆ *This could be another good topic to share with other group members. Or you could ask for help from others in the group who may have some helpful hints about ways you can make modest but meaningful changes in the way you live your life. We are always seeking to improve our quality of lives.*

You may find yourself now thinking more about both your physical house as well as your physical body. How does it feel to have removed so much clutter?

Are there real ways you need to do that as well as the metaphorical ways? Turn all those ideas into *Action Steps* and plans for your future.

I hope that you will be generous in congratulating yourself on a job well done.

◆ *Share with others in the group anything at all—take a risk—and others will certainly benefit.*

Project Two

On Being Present

How to live more in the moment? That is a quest I have had for all of my adult years—how about you? Let's take some time to work on this together. You know the saying, "Yesterday is gone, tomorrow is not yet here and today is a gift—and that's why we call it the *present!*"

My hunch is that looking at how we can live more in each moment can take us into many new directions and opportunities for healing. Our exercises in this project will hinge on this 'being present' theme while veering off into some other considerations as well, like personal power, forgiveness and magic.

You will notice that each session begins with a **Five Minute Sprint**, followed by a *JournalCard*. This is done to help you make the shift from external focus to internal awareness, and is recommended for each time you write. I mention this rationale in each Project, since you may take them out of sequence, and I don't think we can be reminded too often to work patiently with ourselves. In addition, I believe you will find that the **Five Minute Sprint** helps you get settled and grounded and better able to access your inner wisdom and 'magic.' Of course, if you don't have the time, you can go directly to the 'new' exercise—because some writing is always better than none!

Know, too, that you can use a *JournalCard* as your journaling session, leaving the other exercises for another time. Sometimes one card can take you to *just the place in the present* that you need to go! Follow your own instincts and trust your process!

Session 1

I. Begin where you are, writing for just about five minutes. This will help you make the shift from external awareness to inner focus and will ground you into being more present to *yourself.* If you need a question to focus upon just ask, "What's going on?" or "How do I feel?" Beginning where you are is necessary, since it is your *true present.*

II. Now pick a **JournalCard,** or two or three. See what they say to you *right now* about you and life and the struggles and joys you have. Let your pen take you into a conversation with yourself about where you are and how this card relates to you in this moment. (The cards are intended to help pull you *into this moment* and to see with new eyes what is going on right in front of you.)

◆ *Group members can deepen their own feelings by listening to each other talk about how their cards took them into a useful awareness. The "magic" of cards helping us remember what we know becomes more evident, and we can open to more of our inner gifts.*

III. Begin this exercise by getting up and walking around wherever you are. Allow yourself to just breathe into the moment, letting go of 'shoulds' and expectations—and opening to what you see, what you really ***see***. What is showing itself to you? What pops out? And what does it have to tell you? Sit down now and write. Describe your focal point, perhaps softening your eye focus so that what ever is meaningful *at this moment* can just emerge for you. Take your time. Enjoy looking at your surroundings as though you just entered the room for the first time. Describe fully that which jumps out at you. If you want, you could imagine that whatever has caught your attention has a message for you---and give it a voice with which to share it. Write that down. Allow yourself to respond if you choose. This is just another way to get to deeper parts of yourself.

With each of the exercises above, see if you can be playful with the process! And enjoy yourself . . . please. Know, too, that what stands out for you today will be completely different than what shows itself to you another day. (I worked on this yesterday for myself and had a ceramic plate from Italy just kind of jump out at me. It reminded me of the gentle life style of Italy and to not push so hard!)

IV. A *mentor* for living in the present? Do you have one? Who are those folks you admire who seem to be able to bend, dip, leap or just sit back, depending on the situation? Make a brief list of people that you can think of who are good at that, and who really are mentors to you for living in the present. Pick one. Describe this person and what it is that makes them so special and important to you. You might want to close your eyes and imagine them walking toward you. As they get closer and closer you see them more and more clearly. As they get in front of you all the descriptive words come into your mind as you have them completely in focus. Then, as you imagine yourself with them, bring your attention back to yourself and notice how you feel inside being with them. Feel and breathe. Then allow your attention to go back on them, and attend to the energy they carry with them. Let yourself write freely, without concern about 'doing it right' and experience your words tumbling out, describing with much more detail and accuracy than you would have believed possible. When you have completed your description of them you may find that you have questions you want to ask. Write them down . . . and imagine their mentor-like responses to you, letting your pen be the scribe as you write.

This could also be saved for your own writing session, separate from this Project. Know that you can create your own exercises and simply need to pay attention to your questions!

V.   What value do you give to "Living in the Present?" On a scale of 1–10, with 1 being not important at all, to 10 being very important, how do you rate your own feelings about Living in the Present? Pick a number and then write about it!

Circle the level of importance of Living in the Present

1	2	3	4	5	6	7	8	9	10

VI.   Watch yourself as you move through your day and see if you can, afterward, get a sense of how aware, how conscious, how present you have been. Write for about five minutes on this topic. Is this important to you?

VII.   What resistance do you feel toward living more fully in the present? Reflect on your observations from the previous exercise (and hopefully your awareness based on this work). What do you see as getting in the way—or pulling you away, from the present? (For example, old habits, comforting ways of "zoning out," or unhealthy coping mechanisms, gossip, judgment – and what else?). In a class I teach at the local community college we refer to these obstacles as "self-defeating behaviors". After you list those reasons for resisting, pick one primary issue. Then draw three *JournalCards* to help you explore.

- The first card is to represent your current situation.
- The second card suggests some kind of action to take.
- The last card indicates what will happen as you take that *Action Step*.

VIII.   Give yourself time now to reflect on what you have written. **Write yourself an Unsent Letter** of love and support in dealing with whatever is currently going on in your life!

◆ *This could be a good time to write a note to the group reporting your new awareness.*

Session 2

I.   As before, begin where you are. Breathe deeply, and as you exhale let go of tension and frustration . . . and then pick up your pen to write. Just let it move and take you wherever is seems to want to go. For just five minutes.

II.   Now pick a *JournalCard.* Let it give you some help in reminding you of what needs attention in your life right now. Notice how you feel as you read your card and how that carries you more deeply into your 'present'. In some ways living in the present has to do with personal power. I say that because without a sense of who we are it is easy to be pulled this way and that, getting caught in others desires and agendas that can lead us astray from our own sense of focus and direction. Remember that this is a place for you to be fully with yourself as you are, without explanation or defense. Enjoy your present moment as you write.

III.   For this exercise I suggest doing a **Cluster** (brainstorming on paper) that can take you into exploring those qualities you have or would like to develop further, that give you more of a sense of your own power. Another way to think of it is that the more authentic you can be, the more present you can be. As we are comfortable with ourselves, we can better co-exist in the moment with whatever is going on. (As always, you don't have to agree with me. So if your own thinking takes you somewhere else, honor that! *That* is your power!) I suggest that you start with a circle in the center of your page and put within it the phrase *"My authentic Self."* Begin randomly to draw lines from that center circle, adding words or phrases that come to mind in relation to the central topic and drawing a circle around the new word. What you will create is a kind of picture of your Authentic Self. The **Cluster** is a powerful exercise because it does such a good job of combining right and left-brain functions. It helps you to open up even more to your authentic self. When complete you may want to highlight those aspects of your authentic self that are most grounding for you, and you could highlight those qualities that need more work with still another color. Write a few sentences about what, if any, new insights you have as a result of your cluster.

Now . . . let's sprinkle a little *magic* into this writing time! I love magic because it is available to us all, just by shifting our inner focus. And sometimes it also helps us become more effective co-creators in our lives. So, with your friend *magic* at your side . . .

✦ Meditation ✦

*. . . feel those authentic and powerful traits of yours **expanding**. Soften your eyes for a moment, asking for help to see more clearly the person you were born to be—with your personal power at a height greater than you have ever **really experienced** before. Breathe that in . . . just be in the moment (hopefully you are alone and have some quiet within which to savor your special qualities). . . then breathe in again, and **feel** your expansion . . . As you feel your **personal power** grow, become ripe and ready to express, let it tell you about who you are, how you can deal with life even more effectively, and may even tell you what is around the corner in your future. Let this altered consciousness continue as long as you desire—speaking with a stream of consciousness about you, your life and those who you love. Feel your power, and comment to yourself about how it feels to be more deeply embedded in your personal power.*

✦

Create an **Alphapoem** about being your authentic, powerful self, either using the whole alphabet or just the words P.O.W.E.R.F.U.L.S.E.L.F. as the backbone of your poem.

Please don't worry about whether it rhymes . . . and see if you can let it be fun. Here is an example:

Slowly I open

Enjoying the discoveries that come

Lingering with some and forgetting others

Finally coming to rest in the NOW.

V. Create an action plan for yourself to get to know more about your strongest characteristics, and to work on developing those that are languishing. Please make this simple and do-able—perhaps just one or two things you can add to your weekly tasks.

◆ *If you want to share one of those* Action Steps *with one or more people it may help you to remember to follow through . . . only if you want!*

Session 3

I. Begin your session as usual, with writing for **five minutes** about whatever is going on for you *in this moment!* Use your newly developing skills of seeing with new eyes that which is capturing your attention in this moment, without judgment. Letting go of judgment allows for eyes that can see even more clearly.

II. Choose *JournalCards* as usual, letting the cards deepen your connection to yourself. Alternatively, if you desire, choose four cards, weaving the words and concepts into a picture of what is now relevant to your life. Give yourself the assignment to use each word from each card at least three times as you describe your current life situation. You can, if you want, play with this in whatever way works most effectively for you. Remember that you have the freedom to use your *JournalCards* in any way you choose.

As we move about in our lives there are often things from our past that bubble up to the surface, sometimes getting in the way of being "present centered." Some of these *old* things are pleasant, and more often, there are things that don't feel good, remind us of hard times, or bring up emotions that color what's going on right now. In the world of counseling we call that "Unfinished Business." Journal writing is a wonderful way to address these kinds of issues, since we can do the work in private, at our own speed and with our own words. As we address the Unfinished Business we are able to clear it more consciously, thus leaving us more room to again be present in the moment.

III. There is a wonderful technique, developed by Ira Progoff, that can be helpful in uncovering Unfinished Business. It is called **Steppingstones** and allows you to get perspective on your life by noting the important events of your life. For our purposes today, simply take a look at the important life events that have contributed to making you the person you are today. According to Progoff, we should always make the first one *"I was born . . ."* And then proceed with eight to ten more steps. You can simply write phrases, without going into detail about any of these **Steppingstones**. These steps are not good or bad, they are just times in our lives that shaped us into who we are today. Number as you go and see what emerges as you relax and let your history show itself to you...in about twelve steps.

IV. When you have written all your **Steppingstones**, read through them, and pick one that has some energy or a 'charge' to it as you read it (like noticing that you stop breathing when you read it, or feel a knot in your gut . . . or if it brings tears to your eyes). That kind of feeling is an indicator of Unfinished Business.

V. Pick one of those **Steppingstones** that has a charge on it for you, and make it the title for another piece of times writing---for about ten to 15 minutes. As another deepening device for your work, you may want to add after about five minutes is the phrase, "If I were really honest . . ." See if that helps you release more.

As medical intuitive Carolyn Myss says, "When we can rid ourselves of unfinished business we have more energy for living in the *present* available to us. When we 'spend' our energy on the past we have less available for ***now***."

VI. As most of you know, we all need to practice more forgiveness. Forgiveness is for *us*, not for the other person, to help us be free from unwanted feelings, yucky energy and weight from another time. You may have your own feelings, beliefs, attitudes about forgiveness. Take five or ten minutes to write about what you know, how you feel, and what you want to do about forgiveness in your life. Are you good at it? Do you, like me, have some trouble understanding it and how to do it? Just lightly explore forgiveness--to yourself, others, and also receiving forgiveness from others.

VII. Let's now return to **Lists** as a technique for journaling. Make a list of all those from whom you would like to ask forgiveness. Make another list of those you would like (eventually) to forgive, and yet another list of those experiences or actions for which you would like to be forgiven. (Remember your journal is private, so you can 'risk' saying some of those things you've felt but never truly acknowledged.) Go.

VIII. And now, **Write a Prayer**, asking for help with one or more of those issues you have that requires forgiveness. Remember that starting with small ones and building to those that are more difficult is a good idea. It's just like physical exercise. On your first visit to the gym you don't want to start out with the 100-pound weight.

IX. One last suggestion, a kind of **Action Step**, is to create an affirmation, talking to and about yourself, to help you shed those qualities or memories which are no longer good for you to carry. As you put it together, keep it simple and short, so you can repeat it when you are out in nature, by yourself, and more open to the forces that support you. One example might be, "I am open and ready to release the damage of the past, to be more fully authentic and powerful." Or "I release negativity and open to power to help me." You get the idea. Create one. Then, when you have the time (within 48 hours), take a walk by yourself, spending some time repeating your affirmation.

Session 4

I. **Five Minute Sprint**. Begin with where you are. Notice how you feel and what is taking your attention. As you "clear" yourself of that, what emerges before you in the present? What do you see, feel, desire or hope for?

II. *JournalCards*. Pick one or more cards, just letting them help you to see below the surface of your conscious awareness. How do these cards help you to deepen? Enjoy the process of exploration.

We are all so powerful, so blessed and so full of hope. Even if you are feeling less than all those words suggest, see what happens if you take a moment to view all that you are going through, and all you have been through, as just what your soul needed. Experiment with the concept of "praise," and look at everything that happened to you today or yesterday, as a blessing. I'm not suggesting that this is easy, but it offers an almost neck-snapping perspective of what we truly have in front of us.

III. Write about that perspective for now as you review what you have been through in the last month or two. *List each event and then write your gratitude for it, even if it seems odd—like being grateful for losing your wallet.* What happens to your perceptions? Make note of your shift in perspective. Experiment with applying that technique to circumstances as they come up during the week to see what it has to teach you.

IV. **Return to magic**. Since we all have magic (or whatever word fits for you) it seems to me that if we were to invite it to be more active in our lives, that we could enjoy each day that much more. Hope, joy, happiness will be more accessible, especially as we drop fear about how things are 'supposed' to be. So, with that in mind, my suggestion is that you invite the Spirit of Magic (or your guardian angel if you prefer) to show itself to you each day. Write an **Unsent Letter** as an invitation, asking to have 'magic' show itself to you daily. You may allow for a response to your letter if you desire.

V. More Magic.

✦ Meditation ✦

Imagine that you are walking in your favorite, most serene location. Describe it in detail in your journal. . . . Then, as you walk along something on the ground catches your eye. . . . It's. . . . an old lantern. . . . tucked partially behind a bush . . . and you find yourself really curious about it. . . . You reach down and pick it up . . . and immediately feel that it is . . . magical!!! Breathing with awareness, to help you deal with your excitement, you brush away some of the dirt and leaves that were stuck to this old lantern . . . and what should happen but whomp!!! Out comes a figure . . . a . . . modern sophisticated business woman! As she appears, she reaches out her hand to you in a welcoming and warm manner. . . . She is radiant, full of life, clearly aware as to how to make the most of each moment she has. . . . And as you watch her, her clothing changes, now into casual and elegant wear . . . and a few minutes later into rugged hiking attire. . . . She just keeps changing, showing you her many facets and abilities. . . . Soon she speaks to you, with the clearest, most present centered essence that you could ever imagine. She somehow makes you feel . . . good. . . . safe. . . . bright . . . rich . . . and very alive. . . . She says she is here to remind you that while you can and should invite magic into your life, that really you ARE magic and your life is beautiful and deep beyond measure. She supports you and your efforts toward growth and is there as an example for you . . . to help you remember more about who YOU really are. . . . You hear, in your own mind, the soothing, tender sounds of her voice as she speaks to you. . . . Let her speak to you now, but before you do, create your own scene, allowing her to appear to you as she does to YOU describing it all—and her many facets and the variety of roles that she plays. . .

Now write about your thoughts and feelings in this moment, describing as fully as you can the woman who popped out of the lantern. When done, re-read what you've written, *this time substituting "I AM" as you read your description of your magical character.* Enjoy.

VI. Draw *four **JournalCards*** to give yourself hints about these four aspects of your past, present and future:

- Your life mission (based on you're here and now self)
- Your primary gift and challenge
- Your current life—what's going on for you now
- Something coming

Do this exercise with a light hand, knowing that tomorrow your reality will change once again.

VII. Finish by breathing into the moment. Look around. Consider how you feel now. Do you see that you have opened your eyes wider? Do you feel more connected to *now*? Review these exercises from time to time to see how you have opened, deepened and become more fully alive!

Hope, Joy, Inspiration: Finding It, Savoring It, Passing It On

The exercises that I have put together for you in this Project are intended to help give you more focus as you enter in to your therapeutic writing experience. I've discovered in my coaching practice and in many, many face-to-face groups that guidelines help to offer focus while still allowing *lots* of freedom for each individual to go in whatever direction is most pleasing at the moment. You are always invited to veer off into your own creative direction if that seems more meaningful to you. I hope that we all get clearer, this month, about how we find hope, joy and inspiration, so we can adopt even *more* positive habits for our lives.

Session 1

I. **Five Minute Sprint.** My personal preference is to begin each journaling session, by taking a few minutes to unwind from what ever you have been doing, and to give yourself time to get focused and grounded inside yourself. We live most of our lives focused outwardly and so this gives us the chance to 'shift' into an inner focus.

As you take a few moments to breathe and to settle into yourself, consciously relax, and release tensions that may have built up for you during your day. And as you do this initiating exercise consider what you have been holding back from saying, what needs to be looked at, or what you are just dying to dump! Give yourself one to five minutes for this.

II.   I also recommend that after the first exercise you also always take time to pick a ***JournalCard***. I'm saying this so that if you break up the exercises and do them at different times, I think you will get more from them if you do these two preliminary exercises. Of course, that is only my suggestion. When you pick your **JournalCard**, think in terms of what you need to be reminded of in this moment. You'll find your card will point you toward *something* that is a key to your opening up further as you move ahead in the exercises.

◆ *As I've suggested before, this is a great way to share your process with the group. Your card can give both you and the members of the group a quick verbal photo of where you are in your life! Sharing is always up to you.*

Since we are addressing **Hope, Joy, & Inspiration,** I'd like to start with a **Clustering** exercise. Rather than jumping into the positive side, though, let's begin with **Clustering** about those things in our lives that suck energy, enthusiasm, hope and life from us.

III.   So begin your **Cluster** with your focus directed toward those things that zap your energy, dim your hope and enthusiasm. This isn't something you want to censor at all. In fact, practice being more open and honest with yourself. No one else will see it, and it could do you a lot of good to dump more of those feelings.

IV.   And now, to balance that first exercise, *begin a Cluster about those things that help you to remember the joy, hope and inspiration in your life.* Put that circle in the center of your page, fill in your topic and begin! As with the previous exercise, practice being as clear and honest as you can be. Remember to consider the smallest details as you think about what inspires you and brings you hope and joy.

In both of those clusters, *highlight or circle darkly those things over which you have some control.* And even for those things over which you feel you have ***no*** control, ask yourself if you have *choices* about the attitude you have about them.

V. Now, write yourself an **Unsent Letter**, suggesting how you can eliminate some of the life draining parts of your life, and how you can enhance and deepen your life affirming aspects of your life.

◆ *This would be a great time to share with the group any insights or discoveries you may have come across at this time. Even if you have done this sort of exercise before, you will see that your journaling is different, because YOU are different than any time before.*

VI. If you would like to explore a little further you could do another **Cluster**—this time about what *obstacles* you encounter as you try to eliminate those draining and destructive aspects of your life. You could include *all* obstacles, even the ones that come up when you try to add *good and enriching things* into your life, too. (If you are finding that you don't like the **Clustering** technique, you can always replace it with **Lists**, which are an alternative way to brainstorm on paper. Just remember to write quickly, number your ideas as you go along, and allow yourself to repeat.)

Session 2

◆ *If you haven't checked in with the group you might want to take a few moments to do that before starting this next series of exercises. You could talk about the card you chose, what you did or didn't like about exercises (as some have about **Clustering**) and any discoveries you've made. We also would love to have you share favorite quotes or books that you find come to mind as you focus on our current topic.*

I. Start by taking a gentle breath and then letting it go. Do that several times. Then begin to write for one to five minutes about what is going on at this moment. Describe any events or experiences that may have caused you stress during the day. And as you do this exercise consider what you have been holding back from saying, what needs to be looked at, or what you are just dying to dump.

II. When you have finished with the initial exercise, draw a *JournalCard*. When you draw your *JournalCard*, think in terms of what you need to be reminded of in this moment. If the first card does not seem to connect with where you are, you can even use that as a subject about which to journal. Draw one or two more if you feel it will help you to better connect to important issues going on for you now.

◆ *As I've suggested so often, this is a real way to share your process with the group. Your card can give both you and the members of group a quick verbal photo of where you are in your life! Sharing is always up to you.*

III.   **"What inspires you to greater hope and joy?"** Make this the topic for the first of three parts of this exercise, called "Series of Three". I learned it from Kathleen Adams and find it a wonderful and surprising way to move into more depth. The technique we will use—*three times*—is the **AlphaPoem**. In this exercise, we are not going to use the whole alphabet; use only ten letters. You can start anywhere, but for fun, you can begin with the first letter of your first name and continue in alphabetical order from that letter. *(Example: Sue, would be: s, t, u, v, w, x, y, z, a, b.)* You use 'ex' words for 'x' and anything you can think of for 'z.' The idea is to write quickly and not to get caught up in trying to make it rhyme or to make it too perfect. It's easiest to write whole phrases than to use just one word at a time.

IV.   When you have finished the first ten lines of your **Alphapoem** about what inspires you to greater hope and joy, *read over the poem, picking the line that is most meaningful to you. Then, let THAT be the title of your next ten-line poem,* beginning with the letter where you left off in your first poem.

V.   *Repeat the last exercise,* choosing the most vital line of your second **Alphapoem**. Again, make that phrase the title for your last ten-line **Alphapoem**.

VI.   Next, re-read your series of three poems. Then, give yourself at least five minutes to *write and react to what you have written.* Make a list of the feelings that come up for you as you write about what inspires you. Hopefully you will discover some deeper feelings and thoughts as a result of this series of three.

VII.   Next, create a **Dialogue** (written like a script), between yourself and **Joy**. What does **Joy** have to say to you *and you to it?* It may be a bit of a stretch for you, but imagine the **Joy** in the Universe to have a voice with which to speak to you can be very interesting! Explore and *enJOY!*

Session 3

I. As you settle in for this session, write the first **Five Minute Sprint**. Think about what you need to express. What is on your mind at this moment? Just open up and allow that shift to happen as you move more in alignment with your center. Let go of anything that is keeping you from being wholly present. Just let your pen move without thinking too hard.

II. After you finish your initial sprint writing, pick at least one *JournalCard*. Use the card to help you get in tune with your Self. Is there something the card reminds you of that needs your attention? How might this card relate to your own special issues this week? Draw another to see how it may augment or redirect your ideas.

III. **Sentence Stems** is a technique we haven't used much, but can be very powerful. Complete each sentence five times with whatever comes to mind. You'll be surprised at some of your endings. *No censoring!*

- One person whom I find very inspiring is . . .
- (*Write this stem **five times**, finishing each one differently. Do the same for each sentence stem that follows.*)
- I have a great hope that . . .
- In my family, joy was expressed by . . .
- My personal hope for myself is . . .
- If I had ten times more hope it would help me . . .
- With more hope, fear becomes . . .

Make up one or more sentence stems that you think would help you look at some part of your life that isn't encompassed in the six suggestions above.

IV. *Pick one sentence that you completed from the above list and make it the title for a* **Five Minute Sprint**. If you desire, pick another and another. This can be a way to clear out some of the clutter that keeps you from joy—or a way to savor the joy you have even more!

V. In the last exercise you explored some broad perspectives about hope, joy and inspiration. Now imagine that you have lived with greater hope and far less fear for one year. In yet another **Five Minute Sprint**, describe your life now, as though you are making a journal entry and are looking back at your last year.

- How has your life changed?
- What is better?
- How do you look at things now?

VI. Now that you have had time to explore your feelings about adding hope and removing fear, use that information in this exercise: Write yourself an **Unsent Letter**, reminding yourself to look for hope and inspiration each day in some very specific, but small and manageable, way. Consider this your *Action Step* for the week.

◆ *While you are welcome to share with your group members at any time during these exercises, communicating about* Action Steps *could be very helpful in discussing options, opening new doors for some, shifting ways of viewing things for others. Or, talk about how useful the exercises were, what you liked best/least and what additional ideas that you have come up with to share with the group.*

Session 4

I. This is your time to open to all that you are. To begin, take a deep breath and exhale slowly, repeat again, and then again, letting go of more tension with each healing breath, *write for one to five minutes about anything that comes up*. Take this time to dump, say what needs to be said or something that is keeping you from being present. Perhaps it will be a time to describe a new *Joy!*

II. After finishing your first Sprint, it's time to pick a ***JournalCard***. If you have not experimented with more than one card, then allow yourself to try drawing two or more cards this time. The cards you pick will hopefully assist you with further deepening. Follow the questions that lead you in the direction you need to go. Be creative as you see how the cards fit your life and those areas that are calling for more exploration.

Here are some broad questions for you to consider on this subject of Hope, Joy and Inspiration.

- What is the hope, joy, inspiration that you have to share with others?
- How do you feel about sharing with others?
- What are your responsibilities in that regard?

Let's see if these exercises help you think some of these questions through.

III. **List** the ways that you carry your positive attitude with you—or ways you would like to do that so as to help others. Perhaps you have made discoveries during this group process that you now realize you want to share, or will find new ideas that emerge as you write. Make this **List**, a *long* **List**—*up to 50 entries*—numbering as you go, allowing yourself to repeat. Write quickly! No censoring or evaluating but just writing about any way that you see yourself carrying positive energies with you—or wish that you did!

IV. When you last offered a hand to someone else—and could see the light of hope in their eyes—how did you feel? Sort through a few of those times, or imagine one you would like to see happen, finally picking one to focus on more fully. Allow yourself to travel back in time within your mind. Breathe into that place and time. Feel the feelings. See the colors. Smell the smells. Feel the aliveness of the moment. ***Describe all this in great detail in your journal.***

V. Next, use your ***JournalCards*** to help you dream up even more ways to offer yourself and your joy to others. Draw three ***JournalCards***, allowing them to point you in a direction to imagine how you may help offer hope, joy, and inspiration:

- To yourself
- To a friend
- To the world

For each card, *write about what your cards suggest to you about offering help, hope and assistance to yourself or others.* Have some fun as you open to your intuition—that will help you pick just the right card!

VI. Create an *Action Step* that will help you to solidify some of your new awareness into your life. Write it down, including how it feels to be a messenger of Hope and Joy. (Or, how hard it might be to do that, too.)

◆ *Group ideas can be very meaningful…and could even lead you to create a group project to assist someone in your community.*

As you work through these Projects remember....

As with most of our topics, one could write forever about these things, so you will receive some guided journaling exercises to help you channel your thoughts in a more focused way. At the same time we always want to encourage your free, creative and spontaneous expression, so know that you can follow these exercises in any way that you choose—always trusting your own intuition the most to carry you to the places YOU want to explore and express. Trust in self and in your innate ability to know what is best for you is what we hope will be strengthened as you write in your journals with regularity.

◆ *Our experience is that checking in with other group members about responses to the exercises or "JournalCards" that were picked can deepen and enhance the experience of this group immeasurably. Certainly we hope you can make time not only to journal but also to spend some quality time with "friends" acquired through your group.*

Project Four

Strength, Joy, Forgiveness . . . Now!

These exercises will help in looking at where we are, where we have been and where we are headed in our lives. As was expressed before, let them guide you just where *you* need to go, altering directions if necessary, so they work for you.

Session 1

I.   Begin by writing a **Five Minute Sprint** about what is going on in the *now* of your life . . . this moment, big or small, wise or petty. Just let yourself write without judging what you are saying. This is the first part of the process and is an exercise in letting go of the inner critic and just expressing. Notice, as you begin to write, the "shift" that occurs, as you leave your awareness of what is going on in your external life, and begin to turn within. You move your awareness to your inner life. Now you have the chance to deepen into even more clarity about your thoughts and feelings. Write for just five or ten minutes—enough to express yourself, but not so much that you run out of things to say.

II.   Now is the time to use your ***JournalCards*** to help you get in touch with what your unconscious or your intuition wants you to think about. Notice that each card states its purpose in the form of questions, since that is what most people need in order to prepare themselves to open to their own answers. The card you pick—or more than one, if you choose—will help you sharpen your focus. Let the card(s) simply stir you up, so that your life issues appear to you in greater clarity. Then, allow yourself to write. Let the words, picture and questions all roll around in your awareness. Don't try to answer all the questions but just let the card give you a . . . *push* . . . to breathe again and open to your greater wisdom. Spend five or ten minutes doing this.

III.   Do you notice how much more opened up you feel now? Breathe in, feeling that heightened expansiveness. Now start the next writing exercise by simply using the words in the title of our class to *play* with, so to speak. Read on for examples.

For each word, *writing quickly*, write what it makes you think of, such as:

When I think of strength . . . (My response) I think of my grandfather.

Strength is . . . (My response) somewhat easier to experience physically than emotionally.

Write ten responses to each of the following

- "When I think of strength . . ."
- "Forgiveness, to me is . . ."
- "My experience with joy is . . ."

Just allow yourself to write spontaneously without thinking too hard. It's a kind of loosening up exercise you can do to get into your inner world. The technique we are using is **Sentence Stems** , and it is the shortest form of journaling. (This method is best used either when you are feeling stressed, tense, wound up, or, as in this case, as a kind of warm-up exercise.)

Next, you will get to try another exercise that is related, but different enough to give you another perspective. It will only take a few minutes, and will give you a chance to try out a technique we will use several times in this four-session project. It is to write with your non-dominant hand. This is a technique explained in the book ***The Power of Your Other Hand***, by Lucia Capacchione, whom I will quote later.

IV.   So for now, simply let your non-dominant hand write ONE sentence for each word. Experiment to see if something different shows up from this other side of your brain! *It will feel awkward . . . but just allow yourself to breathe into it . . . and go with it.*

V.   When you are finished with experimenting with your other hand, return to putting your pen in your dominant hand and write a few sentences, using all three words. See where you are after this exploration—even if you didn't like it. (Sometimes we learn valuable things even when the exercise isn't "fun.")

VI.   Now, give yourself some time to review the last year. Now that you are "juiced up" after writing quickly in your previous exercises, give yourself time now to make **List** of your *strong* memories from the last year. You will probably notice some areas that call for *forgiveness* to yourself or someone else, and certainly will remember some moments of *joy* as well. Make your list . . . *now!*

VII.   After writing your list, review it. Write a **Five Minute Sprint** responding to the question "What stirs?" This is a favorite question in the work of Ira Progoff, the father of journal therapy, and is a good one to use whenever you are reviewing a series of exercises you have done.

VIII.   Having looked over your list of what your *strong memories* are of the year just past, pick one. Giving yourself time to move yourself back into that experience, practice your descriptive skills by creating a verbal photo of that very strong experience.

IX.   Now, *again using your non-dominant hand*, describe your personal strengths that have been most in play during the last year. Every strength we have has its positive side and its negative side. For instance, I could be very studious, which is good at times, but could show up as isolation, which isn't so good. Which side of your strengths showed up?

Session 2

Before we get in to more writing exercises I want to offer some information from the book mentioned last session, ***The Power of Your Other Hand***, by Lucia Capaccione. It is really very interesting and will help you appreciate even more the experimenting you did in Session 1. Also, it will tend to lead you into more personal experimentation in your everyday journaling. Here is what Lucia has to say:

"In teaching hundreds of people to write with both hands, I've observed over and over that writing done with the *other hand* often expresses the disowned and oppressed parts of the self. With profound simplicity the *other hand* speaks for the powerless, weak, subordinate aspect of the personality. This "silent partner" releases emotions and desires that have been stored away in the unconscious. You may wonder why this is so. The Non-dominant hand is generally considered the *wrong hand* for writing, so it is the *perfect* hand for expressing anything in ourselves that has been judged as wrong.

"Writing with the *other hand* brings up feelings of awkwardness. It is the unschooled hand. Since it has not been trained to write, its handwriting looks like a child's: slow, awkward, clumsy, ugly (by most standards of penmanship). Often the scrawls are barely legible. Spelling errors frequently occur, even among good spellers.

"Almost all the people I've worked with said they felt child-like and vulnerable when they first wrote or printed with the *other hand*. Some people report that primitive and raw emotions came to the surface. The Inner Child frequently comes out in a rush of feeling. And beneath the layers of hidden emotions, one finds an intuitive and creative voice. When you realize that the right hemisphere in most people governs the non-dominant hand, it is no surprise that the qualities ascribed to the right brain—creative, emotional, intuitive—are precisely the qualities that come out most easily when the non-dominant hand writes.

"It is easier to express feelings by writing with the *other hand*. For that reason, it is an excellent therapeutic technique. Scribbling out rage, fear, frustrations, sadness, helplessness, and vulnerability can bring immeasurable relief, both physically and emotionally. It's a wonderful way to reduce stress caused by a build-up of emotions. It's a safe method for letting off steam without hurting anyone or anything. It's a playful way to dump emotions without attacking others or the environment.

"There is energy and life in feelings. The energy doesn't go away simply because those feelings are denied or stuffed down. On the contrary, the bottled-up energy turns rancid and becomes pain, depression, or disease. Thwarted emotions may eventually erupt in verbal outbursts or physical violence. Writing or drawing with the *other hand* allows feelings to come safely to the surface to be acknowledged and accepted."

I hope you found that excerpt from her book interesting. You may be interested in continuing to experiment more with writing with your *other hand,* and to buy the book as well.

I.   Next, allowing yourself to simply write freely for **five minutes** or so, notice what is going on for you. Let your pen move and express just what is uppermost in your mind at this time. Start with one hand . . . and, if you want, move to the other . . . but most importantly for this exercise, as you warm up, be sure that you are comfortable, letting go of any expectations. You may even find it helpful to allow yourself to tear up and throw away your first warm-up. That can help you discard your inner critic and really open up to where you are.

II. Time again to pull a *JournalCard.* Start with a deep breath, feeling your whole body fill as you breathe in, and then exhale. Read over what you have just written in your first exercise and see if you really feel clear and open. If you do, go ahead and pick a card to see how it fits for your life right now. If you don't feel clear, take the concern you have and ask for guidance in that area as you pull the card. See what comes. You may even want to draw another card to help move you into an even deeper space within. Write for as long as you like— 5 to 15 minutes. Remember that you don't have to answer all the questions.

Over the years of working with the *JournalCards* I've realized that sometimes we pick a card that is really pointing us to its opposite. Opposites or polarities are valuable to look at since most of us have experiences that carry us from one site of a polarity to another. My strength may be friendliness, for instance, but it can carry me into co-dependence, which is a weakness. Both may be true, so it is not a judgment, just a clearer view of reality.

III. Consider strengths first. We took time last session to look at personal strengths that were in play in our lives last year. So what are their opposites? What are the weaknesses that were in play last year as well? I bring this up because it helps us to have a richer and more reality based view of ourselves. Make two lists now, one of strengths you have and one of weaknesses. Explore your different aspects and polarities within. No judgment, just observation. It won't take too long, and don't think about it too hard.

This is a perfect lead-in to working more with forgiveness, since when we look at our imperfections we sometimes feel the need to move into self-forgiveness or acceptance. Did that happen for you? Did you reveal things about yourself that you are not happy about? When you described your strong memories of last year were there memories triggered that were difficult or unpleasant? Do these memories help you to get in touch with that which you want to forgive—either in regard to yourself or someone else?

IV.   What, if anything, do you feel a need to forgive now? Consider yourself first and then others. Write about your thoughts and feelings about what or who needs to be forgiven.

V.   From those issues you just identified as needing attention in terms of forgiveness, allow yourself for now to pick one of them to explore further. (You can go through them all when you have the time if you desire.)

VI.   In the next exercise try writing a letter to God, asking for help and guidance with this forgiveness issue. Invite help and assistance so that you may understand better how to proceed. **Unsent Letters** is a great technique that allows us to say just what needs to be said, without censure. Open up and really say it *all*. God, defined as you choose, can deal with whatever you have to say.

VII.   When you have finished your **Unsent Letter**, give yourself a few minutes just to breathe and release. Then, *pick up your pen in your other hand* and allow God to respond to you.

VIII.   Again, using Progoff's question, ask yourself "What stirs?" Take some time to write about your experience and feelings about what has come up for you so far.

Session 3

I.   Begin, as always, with a **Five Minute Sprint, Freewriting** to open yourself up, let go of draining and annoying thoughts, and to make that shift from external focus to internal focus. See if you can continue to take chances as you do this, knowing you can always throw what you have written away if you choose.

II.   Let your **JournalCards** help you now to deepen your awareness of where you are, this time choosing one, two or three cards. Choosing more cards may allow you to put the words together, focusing less on the questions and more on the impressions left upon you by the words, pictures and questions as a totality. Let your intuition carry you into clarity of just what you need to address, with the help of your cards.

Forgiveness, for many if not all of us, is a difficult process. Besides not knowing exactly how to do it, I often find that I need to do it repeatedly—even when I have been convinced that *I really did let go of it!* Know what I mean?

One of my heroes, author, and therapist Stephen Levine, always reminds his readers to start forgiveness, like exercise, with reasonable sized weights rather than beginning with a 100-pound weight—which could be parental issues, abandonment, abuse, ex-spouses or whatever. Better to begin our 'practice' with smaller irritations and aggravations . . . so we build the weight gradually.

Levine also helped me to understand that when we do forgiveness we aren't condoning behavior. We're letting go of the energy of holding on to the resentments we carry. Those energy drainers keep us from living fully, from having energy for the beautiful things that lie all around us. So, when we forgive, we are freeing ourselves, and the negative ties that bind us to other people and times. Of course I don't expect one paragraph to fully explain this process, but rather encourage you to explore more about this topic on your own. Carolyn Myss has some good thoughts on the topic, which you could explore at www.myss.com.

III.   So with all this in mind, make a **List** of *small* things that have used up your time and energy over the last few weeks. As you get clearer about how you do that you will be able to forgive, and 'save' your energy for the many joys that surround us. Sometimes we don't have the ability to see the simple joys, with our energies "dimmed" from anger and resentment. *(Pay attention to how you feel as you write down and release those little irritations, and the space you make available for joy and pleasure—and peace! Feel the space open up as you write!)*

IV.   Can you see now, that as you use your strength and courage on your own behalf—forgiving the small and petty annoyances, that you make room for more of what is pleasing and creates happiness? (I can practically feel it bursting open before me as I am writing this—as I am practicing releasing some of my own anger). Sift through your recent past again, *this time noting everything you can think of that brings you joy.* You can do this in the form of a **List** or **Cluster**.

Honesty is another important aspect of our general health and well-being. No matter what it is that we want to do with our lives, we will come from a clearer and more centered place if we know how to be honest with ourselves. And the journal is a perfect format for that practice—since it is to be kept private and just for our own eyes.

Julia Cameron writes about the need for honesty in writing in her book, **The Right to Write**. Some of the phrases she suggests may work for you in this next exercise. Her suggestions are to begin a sentence and then paragraph with:

"**If I let myself admit it, I** . . ."

"**If it weren't so risky, I'd** . . ."

"**If it didn't scare me, I** . . ."

"**If it weren't so stupid, I'd** . . ."

V. Use one of these phrases as you write honestly about the insight and awareness that surfaced for you as you have done this exercise. Consider your strengths—and their opposites, your weaknesses. Think about what and whom you can and cannot (or will not) forgive. Think, too, about how you might carve out space for more joy and pleasure in your life. Don't try to write about it all, but just focus on that *small* piece that resonates for you right now and spend a little time writing about that. You can always come back and explore more later.

VI. I hope you feel a kind of cleansing after having written honestly about where you are just now. I suggest that you read over what you have just written and pick out words and phrases that stand out for you, that are really "juicy."

- Which phrases give you a sense of movement and forward direction?

- Pick the *best* of those phrases, and make it the title for a **Five Minute Sprint**. Again, use any of Julia Cameron's phrases to help you move into even greater honesty. This series of short sprints is called a "**Series of Three**", and I learned it from Kathleen Adams, who wrote **Journal to the Self**.

- When you have finished with that piece of writing, again pull out the strongest and richest phrases. Pick one again, and make it the title for one more **Five Minute Sprint**. Allow yourself to breathe, open, and *reach in for more and more personal honesty.*

VII. Once again, respond in writing to the question "What stirs?" as you review your experience with the last exercise.

VIII. For fun you may want to now do an **Alphapoem** with *personal honesty* as the phrase you write down the left hand side of your page. Then, using each letter as the first letter of each phrase, write a non-rhyming and spontaneous poem about personal honesty. It should flow easily after your earlier writing.

Session 4

I. Make your **Five Minute Sprint** in this session one in which you address where you are with this process in general, the exercises in particular, and the rest of your life! Notice how you feel, as you honestly evaluate where you are. Do you notice how much easier it is to be honest when there is no one looking over your shoulder?

II. Next, *make a statement or ask a question that summarizes your current focus* in your life presently. Do this honestly, with no holding back. There may be more than one issue going on. Pick and choose what stands out most right now. Then, get your *JournalCards* out. You will pick *four* cards, so pay attention to the order in which you pick them.

- The first card represents some aspect of your strength.
- The second card gives you clues about something in regard to forgiveness.
- Third card will help identify something related to *joy*.
- Fourth card represents the magic of *now* and will influence all the others.

See where these cards take you in reference to your current focus in your life. Again using your attitude of honesty, see how the cards offer you suggestions that you can apply to your situation. Sometimes you have to be creative with your cards . . . so *have fun with this!*

◆ *This could be a great time to share insights with the rest of your group!*

III. Now, let's return to the use of the *other hand* and let *it* now express that which is of most importance as you look ahead in your life. What does this other hand represent? See what happens as you learn from this other hand.

IV. Do your two hands agree on what is most important? If you would like, try creating a **Dialogue** between the two hands...and what they represent in terms of your life focus. It could be very enlightening to explore a conversation between the two!

V.   Using the wisdom now of your combined hands, create three *Action Steps*s–goals of sorts—for what you want to create next in your life. Use your strength, minimize your weakness, offer forgiveness to yourself and others, and begin to make room for more *joy* in each new *now* that you encounter.

◆ *Another good time to talk within the group about goals, as well as other things that you have learned in the process of this Project. As you share, your lessons may become even more meaningful.*

Project Five

Get a Grip!
A Health Perspective

I've discovered in my face-to-face groups that guidelines help to offer focus, while still allowing *lots* of freedom for each individual to go in their own direction. You are always invited to veer off into your own creative direction if that seems more meaningful to you. I hope that we all get clearer, this month, about our health values, so we can adopt even more positive habits for our lives.

◆ *As group members share their experiences, there is room for talking about the* ***JournalCards*** *you have drawn, responses to particular exercises, as well as sharing about how difficult it may be to get yourself time to actually DO the exercises. I think you'll find that the group responds in a warm, loving and supportive way. Feel free to ask questions, make comments and to enjoy this new kind of Group experience!*

Session 1

I. Begin your journaling time by taking a few minutes to settle into the space you've created for your journaling time. Stretch and breathe before you begin, and allow yourself time to make the shift from outer awareness to inner focus. You may want to just ask yourself to begin to write and watch your pen carry you forward, or ask a question like, "What's going on?" to get started. Write (really) for just about **five minutes**. This is just a warm up.

II. The **JournalCards** are part of the deepening process you go through as you do this writing. Shuffle your cards and fan them out so you can pick *just* the card that fits for you today. As you do that your own intuition is acting and helping you get a card that can remind you of important issues in your life currently. Let the card just "stir you up" so you can tune in to some aspect of your life to write about. After you have gotten used to the cards you may want to pick one or two more to add substance to the first card. It's fun to play with them to see what kind of questions emerge for you!

You can write as long as you want after pulling your cards, but if you want to remain "contained" in your writing process, you could experiment again with just writing for five minutes. It's sometimes good to know that you *can* say something meaningful for yourself in such a short amount of time.

III. Now it's time for another **"Steppingstone"** exercise from Ira Progoff's work, one that will allow you to think about your feelings, attitudes and beliefs about *health* throughout your life. The first step begins with "I was born . . ." and then is followed by 10 or 11 additional steps. What would they be?

This exercise gives you a chance to think about your health throughout your life. The steps are neither positive nor negative, just what you remember about your experience. For instance, the next step that comes to me is that of breaking my leg when I was four years old. That's all that needs to be said at this point—just a descriptive line. And make only 10–12 health-related steps for your whole life. So take a deep breath, begin numbering your page, and see what memories come up for you. It's valuable to realize that this specific exercise is meant just to consider what comes up for you now; if you did the exercise a different day you might have different memories, so don't think too hard. Come back for additional instructions when you are done!

IV. Okay, now that you have completed your **Steppingstones**, you can read through them. Notice, as you do, which ones still have a "charge" on them—leave you with some sort of emotional feeling? One of my steps could be something like "I felt somewhat arrogant about my good health"—and that leaves a "charge" for me now. Those feelings are examples of "unfinished business" perhaps—or at least unexpressed emotions. Pick just one of your **Steppingstones** and use it as a title for another **Five Minute Sprint**!

V. Next, I want to suggest to you that you begin a **Dialogue** *with your body!* In order to do this, simply need to imagine that your physical body has its own voice, and can speak to you. Either side of the **Dialogue** can begin, and it's easiest to begin with a question, like, "Body, how do you feel about the way that I feed you? Do you like what I eat or would you rather I make some changes?" or, "How healthy do you feel these days, body?" Of course, you will probably have your own questions, so just go with what is comfortable and comes easily to you.

Write the **Dialogue** as though you were writing a script. If you want to add in another dimension, use your non-dominant hand to write your body's response. Take this conversation as far as it will go. When you are through you may want to read it over and make a few notes about how you feel about what was said.

◆ *Check in with your group and share what you want.*

Session 2

I. Begin again, with a short piece of writing that is just about whatever is going on with you in the moment. This is always a good way to begin, and also good to limit to about **five minutes**. Each exercise takes you first from the here and now, to deeper and deeper parts of yourself. So, take a deep breath and begin.

II. Now that you are more focused on yourself and your writing, allow yourself to again choose "***JournalCards***." As your unconscious helps you to look into your life by focusing on a card, see what comes up. Again, allow it to "stir" you, and see how the card you picked helps you to loosen up some thoughts about something going on in your life. Go for about five minutes. Again, if you feel like picking another card, and even another to support the first, feel free.

◆ *This is still a great way to check in with the group—to tell them what card you have chosen at the beginning of this session's work.*

III. In this case, since our topic is about our health perspectives, I want to suggest that you do your **Cluster** on the topic "Actions in support of my health." What are the things that you do—or think that you should do, to support your health? Allow yourself to brainstorm—so write quickly, without judging or censoring what you are writing.

Stretch a little and put things in there that you think would be healthy even if you don't yet do them. Begin!

Now, if you want, you can use different colored pens to highlight those things you *do* and those you *want to do.*

IV. Write a few sentences about what you learned from this exercise.

V. And now here's another idea for some fun. Find an envelope—any size you want. Let it represent your body——and you are going to take care of it by decorating the outside in a caring and loving way, and then as you think of it, adding things that you want to put *inside* your envelope, inside your *self,* as you go through your week. So just take some time to get out some crayons or markers and decorate your envelope. Remember that you are *divine,* so make your decorations accordingly!

◆ *Please share your experience with these exercises with the group!*

Session 3

I. Begin again with a deep breath and a good stretch. Then just begin to write about what ever is foremost in your mind at this time. Remember that this is the 'shift' from outer to inner, and so just "go with it!" Write for about **five minutes** and notice your focus moving from outside to inside.

II. And now get your ***JournalCards*** out again, to help you get in tune with your own consciousness. Take a deep breath, and spread out your cards in front of you. What needs some attention? How might this card relate to your own health issues this week? In what ways does it tell you that you need to be reminded?

III. Obstacles. We all encounter obstacles to taking care of ourselves best. What are your stumbling blocks? These could range from not taking enough time to exercise to not fully understanding a disease that is attacking your body.

Make a **List**—as long as you can, of all those obstacles you encounter when you try to live in a healthy way. Number as you go, and allow yourself to repeat. Write quickly and you'll have better luck in opening up your unconscious. *Make a list to 25 even if you think you are very repetitive.*

When you are through your list, notice which obstacles were written more than once, perhaps even in slightly different language. Those obstacles may represent greater concerns for you right now, and may be the ones you want to address first. Look through your list and find one that you would like to examine more deeply, being aware of those over which you do have some control and those over which you do not have control.

IV.   Pick one of those obstacles now as you move into the next exercise. Using your **JournalCards** again. Pick three cards:

- The first one will give you some insight into this obstacle and how it relates to your life now.
- The second card will suggest in some way, how you can take action to deal with your obstacle.
- The third card will give you an idea of how your life can shift once you have taken necessary action.

See how these cards might help stimulate ideas for you that will help you see beyond your current "stuck-ness". Write about what comes as you see each card giving you new direction.

You may want to experiment with other obstacles that you realize keep you from a healthy lifestyle, and see how your cards might help you come up with creative and "out of the box" ways to improve your healthful living.

V.   What stirs? Take a few minutes to respond to this general question… and then consider all the awareness that has come up as you wrote about these topics.

Session 4

I.   Begin as usual, taking a moment to focus and breathe deeply, and then just begin to write a **Five Minute Sprint**. Notice the inner shift you make as you take your focus away from externals and into your life. Enjoy the release as you "dump" those feelings that you don't need to carry around any more!

II.   Choose a **JournalCard** to help you move a little deeper, and see where it takes you today. Where is your focus and what is important to your right now? Let your card start you off, and then proceed in your own direction, asking more of your own questions as you go.

Come back to them later to give you additional direction to your journaling.

III. Let's check back in with what the body has to say to you now, and you to it. After spending the last three weeks with some focus on health and healthy activities, is there something you want to say to your body?

IV. Begin by writing an **Unsent Letter** to your body, telling it how you feel about it, what new insights you have gained and what you hope to do in the future, which hopefully starts soon. When you have done that, allow yourself to take a deep breath, and allow your body to respond. You may continue then, turning it into a **Dialogue** if you like.

V. Guided Meditation to be with your *Inner Healer*. Give yourself some time to be quiet and without disturbances. If you have someone who can read this to you, or if you can record it you will enjoy it that much more. If not, just read it slowly, breathing frequently as you read, and allow yourself to respond when finished.

✦ Meditation ✦

You are going to move into a gentle and relaxed space now. As you read this you feel your muscles relaxing and know that this is a good thing, . . . There is nothing that you have to do now in the way of performing . . . but only need to open and receive that which is available to you at any time . . .. The difference now is that you are opening to receive, and to receive from that very wise, deep and wonderful part of yourself that is a true and loving HEALER. You needn't know on a conscious level just how you get to this very special and magical part of yourself, but only need to believe that you are being guided there. Your spiritual helpers, however you experience them, are at your side now, helping you identify this rich and wise aspect of yourself. You may want to now go DEEPER into yourself, feeling the safety and desirability of turning to this wise part of yourself. Your healer is gentle and calm and loving, like the best healer you have ever met, and you begin, just by moving closer to your healer, knowing that you are opening into warmth, love and help. Allow yourself just to bask in the glow of the space that you now enter. Be quiet there. Absorb the goodness. Allow yourself to receive. If you see a figure, ask it questions, or if you just enjoy how this space feels, just feel. Whatever comes to you is just what you need to experience now. Move further into this healing space. Ask for help in any way that you wish . . . know that just what you want and need will come to you in just the right way . . . Stay in this space as long as you desire . . . .. Sit in the stillness and beauty . . . Trust . . . .. Release . . . Forgive . . . Accept . . . .. Smile . . . .

✦

As you feel ready, you can move away from your *Inner Healer*, still carrying with you the energy you gained in the encounter. Allow the healing in. When you are ready, take a deep breath, pick up your pen, and begin to put words onto paper about this special experience.

VI.   Create *Action Steps* based on your work this month to be more honoring and loving to your body and soul, little by little. I encourage you to keep up with your journal, to keep track of how you feel and what you are doing. Continue to use the cards each time you sit down to journal…and let them give you focus until you shift into your own healing space where you know exactly what needs to be said and done.

I wish you well . . . and wellness.

Project Six

Moving Forward
With Faith, Friendship and Fun!

If you been taking on these Projects one at a time and in order, you've noted that we follow a pattern, beginning with a short piece of writing in the moment (the **Five Minute Sprint**), followed by *JournalCards*, and then more exercises specifically geared to the topic. Hope you enjoy this one, too! So . . .

Session 1

I.   Jump in with a **Five Minute Sprint**. It is, as it sounds, writing for five minutes. It's a great way to transition from our focus on what is going on outside of ourselves to what is going on inside. Write about whatever you want to, whatever is in your mind right now. Don't expect wise or clever or bright words. In fact, simply give yourself unconditional permission to write about anything at all. As you move into this writing you'll begin to feel the shift to greater inner awareness. It's important to remind yourself that there are no rules for journaling, so you cannot do it incorrectly. Write, if you want, about something that you have not said that needs to come out. *Just begin.*

II. Now, having begun that internal shift, draw one or two *JournalCards*, thinking as you do about what you want to be reminded of as you take time for yourself to think about your life and moving forward. Just allow yourself to be 'stirred' by the cards. Let them stimulate a response that fits your life. As you are getting used to them, feel free to pick two cards and then use the one that resonates best for you. Again, take only about **five minutes**. You probably won't be able to answer all of the questions, but don't worry about that. If you find that you'd like to continue writing until all of them are answered, that's okay, too!

◆ *After any of these exercises you may want to talk with your group about your experience. Feel free to do that—it makes the group process lots of fun. Sharing your* **JournalCard** *and how it does or doesn't fit for you helps the group to know you more, too.*

III.   Remember, there is no right or wrong way to do this project, so simply take another five minutes, now, to react in writing to the title of this Project, "**Moving Forward with Faith, Friendship And Fun**." What do all those "F" words bring up for you? Journaling gives you the freedom to establish your own values about what is important to you, so how do you relate to these words—and how might they impact you and your life?

Do you notice how you have already moved into more depth?

We will enter into the following four sessions gently and playfully. In the first session we are going to use the **JournalCards** again—in a different way than before. It's a way of giving yourself an overview of your life—lots of fun, really, to see what is brought into your line of vision.

This exercise will give you a chance to playfully examine just what *is* important to you, as you move forward in your life, whether it is what the cards suggest or what you realize they have left out! *This can be a useful exercise to return to anytime you feel the need for some renewed perspective.*

IV.   Ready? Shuffle your deck of **JournalCards**. Then draw *four* cards. Pay attention to the order in which they are chosen. Let each card fall into one of the following four categories

- First card: Current life mission;
- Second card: The gift and challenge you have been given;
- Third card: The here and now situation; and
- Fourth card: Something that is coming in the future.

Just breathe into each card and see how it could be pointing to something going on in your life. Play with it! Don't get too serious about it—but enjoy the synchronicity of the cards you choose. You can take just as long with each card as you desire. Know that the more time you spend with them the more connections you will make, and the deeper they will take you.

◆ *This, too, could be fun to share with the larger group. How do your cards fit with your overall understanding of how you are moving forward in your life? Does it help you? Does it bring up more questions? Write down your questions—those are your journaling prompts that you are creating for yourself.*

Session 2

I. Begin again by writing for 1 to 5 minutes about anything at all (**Five Minute Sprint**). Before you actually write you may want to briefly close your eyes, take a deep breath, release, and do that again. If a question or statement forms for you, write it down and respond. If not, simply begin with "What's going on for me now?"

II. As you continue this shift of focus from outside of yourself to inside yourself, prepare to pull a ***JournalCard***. This time, breathe and draw a card, asking for guidance perfect for this moment. You many want to read over the card to see where it takes you—and if you desire, pull another card, allowing it to augment and deepen the theme suggested in your first card. See what works best for you.

This session is about Faith and what that means to you. Faith is an important word because it speaks to what we hold dear and to what keeps us grounded. In today's world, it makes sense to consider where we put our faith and how we rely upon it.

III. First, finish these sentence completions (the shortest form of journaling techniques):

- I have faith that . . .
- One of the things I do faithfully is . . .
- My faith helps me . . .
- I put my greatest faith in . . .
- I want more faith to help me . . .
- One thing I have no faith in is . . .

I hope that by completing these sentences and any other phrases about faith that come to you, that you will begin to bring the meaning of the word more into focus. When I was in college I read a book called ***Dynamics of Faith***, by Paul Tillich. He wrote:

*"Faith is the state of being ultimately concerned: the dynamics of
faith are the dynamics of man's ultimate concern."*

You may or may not agree, but what he suggests is that we have faith in that which we find most important—that about which we have *ultimate concern*. When I was a young student I found this to be a fascinating way of looking at faith and why people choose to operate from different sets of values.

IV. For this exercise I would like you to continue exploring your own faith by making a list of those things about which you are "ultimately concerned." See if they match up with what you *think* you have faith in. Or, what *is* your definition of faith? How does it serve you—or not? How does faith enter in to your life? After writing for a few minutes on this topic, add the phrase, "If I were really honest . . ." and see where it takes you. (This phrase is a good one to throw in no matter what you are writing about, and will immediately take you in to greater depth.)

◆ *The bottom line of this exploration is for you to consider what you believe in—and how it helps you as you move forward in your life. See what part of this piece you feel comfortable sharing with your group.*

V. Now, go back to the exercise you just completed. As you read through it, *underline the key words and phrases that speak to you.* As you then look over those selections, pick one phrase that is the "juiciest," the one that has the most emotion, energy, or interest for you within it. Use that phrase as the title for a special **Alphapoem.** In this case, you'll use the word **FAITH** as the spine of your poem. Use each letter as the first letter of the first word of each line:

F

A

I

T

H

After you have written that poem, again choose a line or a phrase that is most meaningful to you. Let that be the title for another **Alphapoem**, this time using the word, **VALUES**.

V
A
L
U
E
S

After finishing that poem repeat this process once again, choosing the most powerful line from the second poem as the title of the third. Use the word **BELIEF** as the backbone of this final poem.

B
E
L
I
E
F

VI. Read over what you have just written and write a response to the Progoff question you've worked with before: "What stirs?" What, if anything, has this set of exercises done to help you refocus on your faith?

Session 3

I. This time, begin again with some deep and gentle breathing, letting go of unwanted tension and stress, creating a calm, comfortable atmosphere before you write. Now, pick up your pen and begin a **Five Minute Sprint** about how you feel in the moment. Keep your pen moving. You could even experiment with scribbling or drawing or writing gibberish—so that you focus less on the words and more on your internal experience. Stay with this for the entire five minutes, then do a little more deep breathing. Notice how you feel.

II.   Next, shuffle your ***JournalCards***, letting your consciousness bring you to a sense of peace and openness. Invite a card to emerge for you that will help you move forward in just the way you need it to, here and now. If you wish, you can draw a second card (to add to your understanding and to deepen the feelings that come from the first). If you still don't feel complete, draw yet another card, then make a short **List** of people in your life (now and earlier) who have been significant in terms of friendship and have impacted you in important ways. Don't limit yourself to the positive influences; include those who have had a negative impact, as well. Do not make this the be-all and end-all of lists. Give it a couple of minutes, then stop, even if you're not quite done. You can always come back and complete your list and your comments later.

- Write one or two descriptive words next to each person's name, words that best describe your feelings and relationship with this person.

III.   Now, using some or all of the words from your list, write a story about *the great gifts and great challenges* of friendship. You have lots of creative choice here. For instance, you might choose to exaggerate your reality. Or you could describe one challenging friendship in your life. Or, you could simply describe, in a sort of essay, the general gifts and challenges of friendship. Don't get caught up in the format—and remember that this is still journaling—so spelling, grammar, punctuation, and structure are not important. My hope is that you will enjoy the time and increased awareness you develop about both being a friend and having friendships.

IV.   When you're through with your story, take a moment to think about *how you are as a friend*, the gifts and challenges you bring to yourself in friendship. Write an **Unsent Letter** asking yourself for greater friendship with ***you***. Decide upon—and write down—at least one concrete step that you can take toward that in your daily life.

◆ *Perhaps you can share your* Action Step *with the group—-as well as any discoveries you made about being and having friends.*

Session 4

I. This time, use some crayons or markers instead of a pen or pencil, so you can play in your journal with this beginning piece of writing/drawing/doodling. Do your **Five Minute Sprint** by experimenting with opening to more fun, joy and playfulness. That's our theme for this session. So have fun with colors, torn paper, or silly words as you get underway.

II. Take a deep breath now, and as you exhale, make a *noise*, releasing tension and stress! (Jot down in your journal a description of your sound and what it was like to express it!)

III. Asking for guidance and directions about adding more fun, joy and play to your life, draw a *JournalCard*—then another—and then another! From the *three*, pick the one that feels like it would be the most *fun* to write about.

IV. Now get out your calendar or planner and designate dates—as many as you can reasonably set over the next one, two or three months—to have fun. This is serious! Ha! We need to *plan* to have fun, sometimes. This is similar to the "Artist Dates" that Julia Cameron talks about in **The Artist's Way**. Before you start picking dates you might want to make a **List** (a long one, I hope) of those people, places, events and things that you experience as the most fun. Use your whole life (including childhood) as your experiential background for this. Once your long **List** is done, begin marking fun dates on your calendar.

V. Now, with your "fun list" done and a schedule established, give yourself time to ponder how you feel about having fun, then write about the process you just completed. Was it easy and fun to do? Was it difficult to do, perhaps not too pleasant even though it was all about fun? Are you already afraid that life will get in the way of your having all that fun to come? Write about those fears of obstacles. Cap it all off with a few thoughts about the best/worst aspects of taking time for fun.

VI. At times, it's useful for us to check in with our friends to help us remember what is important. Which of your friends are good at having fun? Whom could you turn to for help in exploring fun times? Perhaps you just need to imagine your friendly Guardian Angel sitting on your shoulder offering her help. Write an

Unsent Letter, as though it is from your Guardian Angel, telling you *why* it's important to you to make time for fun in your life.

VII. Look back over your journaling related to this entire process. What stands out for you? Do you have more clarity about how you want to move forward? Does your faith support you? Where do you stand with friendships? And is there enough fun in your life? Of course, there may be more that needs to be considered as you move ahead, so make note of that as well, and write about it if you wish.

VIII. As a way of pulling all of this together, gather up some old magazines, old journals, pictures, markers, and colored paper. With scissors, paper and glue, create a *collage* of the life you want to have as you move forward. Spend some time on this, and put your feelings into it. Create a *vision* for the next phase of your life. When you are done, put your collage up on a wall (or on your refrigerator) so it can be a steady reminder to you, both of what you want and of the power you have to make it so!

Spring Cleaning for the Spirit!

Whether you are doing these projects in order or are just selecting them at random, here's another chance to explore and deepen your sense of inner wisdom and "magic." I also hope that you have been to my website by now (www.journalmagic.com) and that you have shared some of your insights at the **Discussion Forum.**

Part of the joy of journal writing is that there are no rules about how it is supposed to be done, and so you can only do it right. Of course, that is part of the safety of using a journal—it is for you alone and for no one else. You can say whatever you need to say at any given time, knowing that in a half hour those feelings might change.

And speaking of change, it may also be helpful to use a journaling book from which you can remove pages at any time. Who knows? When you change your mind you may also want to "erase" the old thinking by taking out passages or whole pages of prior writing. It is **not** a requirement that each page be kept—so give yourself permission at times to say even those ugly things that you would not want anyone to hear, and then if necessary, rip those pages out (even better, burn them!).

What is most important of all is that we write out and *express* how we feel in that moment when we are journaling.

While going through the exercises throughout this book, know that they are only suggestions and if you would rather go in a different direction, then go there. Your feelings and your creative release are ultimately what are most important.

◆ *If you are going through these classes with a group, feel free to share your discoveries as you go. If there are any questions that arise for you at any time as you proceed, be sure to ask them.*

You may find it helpful to do these exercises over again in six months to a year. You will have a very different experience each time.

Spring Cleaning for the Spirit

What this title means exactly will be up to you to decide. I think we all have some sense of "spring cleaning." My perspective is that the Spirit in each one of us is the perfect representation of who we are: our essence, our soul, our connection to the Divine.

For whatever reason, we sometimes cover up, dislocate or distract ourselves from our greatest Truth. "Spring Cleaning" helps us to explore what has dimmed our Spirit and allows our inner perfection to shine through. As we go through that "shining and buffing experience" we'll hopefully be better able to know what we want and where we are going.

Imagine a new ***JournalCard*** about *Spirit.* Here's my version, offered here as a way to move into some thinking about what we each mean by Spirit. See where these questions take you.

- "Spirit shows itself to me in . . . ?" Finish that sentence in as many ways as you can.

- How has your life been touched by a relationship with spirit, however you may describe it? Write significant steps of your spiritual growth from 1 to 12, beginning with "I was born . . ."

- What are the questions you have that you would pose to Spirit? Make a list of them. Ask one question, take a deep breath, and write the response as though from Spirit—with your non-dominant hand.

- The warmth, love and compassion of Spirit now wants you to know that . . .

Feel free to use those questions now, or at another time, to further explore your relationship with Spirit.

Session 1

I. As usual, let's begin with a short piece of writing (**Five Minute Sprint**) to help create the "shift" from awareness of your external life to your life internally. This "shift" often seems elusive as our culture presents us with more and more distractions, so this exercise is particularly useful (and can be used anytime you need to gain a sense of being more centered and balanced). In this context, you can allow yourself to be as scattered or focused as you feel. There are no judgments here, no "requirements." Where are you now as you begin, and how do you feel? Just let your pen move and see what comes out.

II. *JournalCards!* Once again, pick a card, and then another, using the questions to help you increase your focus and move into unexplored and interesting parts of your psyche!

◆ *This is usually a good time to share with other group members if you haven't already. Tell them what cards you chose and how they did or didn't help you to turn further within.*

III. Next, we'll tiptoe into our topic. Begin by simply responding to this title "Spring Cleaning for the Spirit." Consider what it was that attracted you to the title. Allow yourself to be light as you respond, trusting that your attention and awareness will deepen as you move from one exercise to another. We spiral down into our depths as we go. What does "Spring Cleaning for the Spirit" suggest to you? Allow your helping angel voices to whisper in your ear as you write about what you want for yourself just now. (Try staying with a **Five Minute Sprint** for this exercise.)

Spring cleaning—really, all cleaning—is a challenge for me. I have a great tendency to put it off, to find other things that are "more important" to do. Yet, no matter how long I procrastinate, the cleaning still needs to be done, and when it *is* done I always feel better. Physical cleaning can help us energetically to feel better internally, so if you have some *real* physical cleaning that needs to be done you may want to make a list of those needs—with dates next to them for when you (or someone) is going to get them done.

IV. Another writing exercise: do some *pretending*. Let's pretend that your huge spring cleaning project has just been completed. You look around, outside as well as inside yourself, and you see all that has been accomplished. You begin to reflect on everything you went through to get to here—but mostly notice how you *feel*. Do you notice a new knowing and new clarity?

Take some time, now, to write your *imagined* journal entry, as though you are already done with this session, aware that all you needed to clean out, both on the inside and outside of you, has now been completed for this season. What do you imagine it is like? (This will be fun to use later as you compare it to your writing at the end of our four-session experience.)

So, as we move further into this topic, can you see that we're dealing with those ways that our Spirit has been dimmed? Why do we not all shine as brightly as we were created to? We need to keep our own Spirits shining, but often that doesn't happen because we are caught up in trying to take care of other people's needs and other levels of "business." If we do take care of ourselves properly, then our Spirit *will* shine forth. We then have our very *best* qualities to share with those we love.

V.   First, do some brainstorming about what keeps you from buffing and brightening your inner Spirit. How do you block your own inner light? What keeps you from being most powerfully yourself? What gets in the way of you being authentically you?

One way to do this is as a **Clustering** exercise (where you draw a circle in the center of your page and write your topic in it). Then ask this question: What keeps you from letting your light shine? Just brainstorm—not censoring or judging, but just letting your thoughts fly.

If you don't like **Clustering** as a technique you can always make a **List,** writing quickly and allowing yourself to repeat. The more quickly you go (whichever technique you use), the more likely you will be to uncover more unconscious beliefs.

My own example for things that keep me from "glowing" has to do with a bit of an 'addiction' to being busy and feeling creative. I push beyond what is healthy, trying to do too much—this work, babysitting for grandchildren, counseling my kids, assisting friends—too often without adequate boundaries.

Now that you have taken a look and become more aware of the ways you keep yourself tied up, write a sentence or two about what you've learned about yourself. It will just take a minute.

VI.   Since we are following this metaphor for Spring cleaning, why not take some time to consider the tools you use for your cleaning? To clean our house we use vacuums, mops, clothes, buckets of water, etc.

What are the creative tools that you can use to get yourself refocused and re-centered? What are your Spring cleaning *tools* for your Spirit? Besides journaling, what else helps you?

VII.   As your final exercise for this session of journaling I want to suggest an **Alphapoem**. This time, use the whole alphabet. Down the left side of your page, write each letter on a separate line, and use each letter as the first letter of the first word of each line of your poem. Write about how ***you*** hope to clear and clean your Spirit through this project. Personalize the topic for yourself so you can proceed with even more clarity as you prepare for the next session!

Session 2

I hope you've had a rich and fulfilling experience so far! You might want to consider jotting down on your calendar each day how "Spirit filled" you felt. Use a scale of 1 to 10, letting 1 represent *not at all* and 10 represent *extremely so*! It is simply another way to track how you feel—-and to give you more of a sense of control over your quality of life.

And, here's a quote from Ken Wilbur to let roll around in your head, too!

> "If we—you and I—are to further the evolution of mankind, and not just reap the benefit of past humanities struggles, if we are to contribute to evolution and not merely siphon it off, if we are to help the overcoming of our self-alienation from Spirit and not merely perpetuate it, then meditation—or a similar and truly contemplative practice—becomes an absolute ethical imperative, a new categorical imperative.. . . . Meditation is simply what an individual at this present stage of average-mode consciousness has to do in order to go beyond that stage in his or her own case."

Wow, isn't that something? Let's move on.

I.   Let's begin journaling, as always, by registering where you are and how you feel. What's going on in your life at this moment? What are you aware of, distracted by or focused upon? No judgment as you write and move into more awareness of your interior self. About **five minutes** of writing is all you need to help you make this shift. If you choose to write more, feel free.

II.   As you use your **_JournalCards_** again, to move into more personal awareness and more depth, you may want to experiment with them. You can always pull them simply to see what shows up, or, if you want to be adventurous, ask as you pick them, "What will best enable my 'Spring cleaning?" See what shows up! Or, you could choose three cards and look at them individually, or combine their message for greater depth. Have fun as you play with them—and always remember that they are used to help you identify how they might fit into your life—it's not that you have to fit your life to the cards.

Those of us who take responsibility for ourselves probably most often return to our own frailties when we look at what gets in the way of our being more alive and authentically ourselves. At the same time, we can look around and see situations, people, beliefs, and attitudes that _do_ contribute to our internal "clutter." Sometimes there are the "stuffed" words we didn't say, the ones that are "stuck" and need release. And there may be entire beliefs, long-held, that no longer fit and need to be dumped or revamped.

III.   With that in mind, make a **List** now, off the top of your head, of all those people and situations with whom you have been entangled and now want release and relief. Make a **List** of all the hassles, beliefs, behaviors, unsaid angers that you can think of, that need to be released. These could be recent contacts or things left from long ago. Just write fast and make your **List** as long as you need to.

IV.   Since this is "Spring cleaning" we are cleaning more deeply than we do on a weekly basis. For your purposes here, read over your last **List** carefully. Mark those pieces you _most_ want to release—at least three, with a star. Write three separate **Unsent Letters** to whomever or whatever you want to release, even if it is an inanimate object or an old belief. Say what you need to say, letting your authentic and blocked feelings out. Be bold and brave! Be honest—and then even more honest. Dig _deep_, as though cleaning in some _really_ hard-to-get-to places. Push yourself a little further than usual. When you're done, if you feel you need to, add the step of burning or tearing up your letters. _Getting those feelings out of you and no longer holding on to them is what is important!_

Whew! Good work! Now, give yourself at least five minutes to just sit quietly and meditate as you say, "Welcome, Spirit" over and over in your mind. Choose another mantra if you desire, but always with the goal of relaxing and releasing even more than before.

V.   Okay, you've been working hard, pushing old, inner 'furniture' around. How do you feel? How do things look within and around you? I have a feeling there may be more for you to release. Is there? Come on, get even more honest with yourself. How about dumping some old beliefs that keep you from being all that you are? Think about self-esteem and whether you support *you* as completely as you would your best friend? If not, what are the beliefs that are holding you back? What achievements have you not accomplished that you believe you could have by now? What beliefs are holding you back? Write about *all* the beliefs that no longer work for you for five minutes. Even if there are only a few, they are probably powerful ones. Take all the time you need to write about this. You may need quite a bit!

VI.   Good for you! Now read over what you have written in the last exercise and underline key phrases, the ones that are 'juicy' and 'speak to you' as being true. Pick *one* and make it the title for another **Five Minute Sprint**. Write about it for five more minutes.

- Do the same thing again, reading over your second **Five Minute Sprint**. Do you see how, by picking out the most vibrant phrase, that you can deepen your views, learning even more about yourself and what you most need to do to help you clean out your psyche?
- Pick again, using the best phrase as the title for another **Five Minute Sprint**.

VII.   What stirs? Read over your **Series of Three** and see what comes to you as you read over *your own inner wisdom!* Appreciate your depth and the resources you have within that you so often leave untapped!

Be gentle with yourself . . . and don't forget to mark your calendar, rating your Spirit-filled days!

Session 3

Happy New Day, journal fan! I hope you have felt more clear and authentic more often in recent days. And it's not too late to track your days on your calendar or planner . . . just an interesting view to see how you are doing.

While we are actively in the process of our Spring cleaning, we are throwing things out and shining up what we like. It's such a simple approach, and a wonder we don't do it all the time. Let's get busy again, as we start another session.

I.   Check in with yourself and make your "shift" into inner awareness as you put your pen to paper and begin to write (**Five Minute Sprint**) about where you are, how you feel, and how you are being pushed and pulled (or fluffed and pampered) in your life right now. Just enjoy what comes from your fingers, through your pen, and on to the paper. In fact, consider enjoying the *process* of writing with less concern about your words, as you write.

II.   *JournalCards* can be chosen one at a time, or you may select several. If you have one particular issue that is bugging you, try picking three *JournalCards*: one for the current situation, one for an action to take, and a third for a view of the newly-evolved situation.

◆ *Working within a group? Report on what comes up for you with the rest of the group!*

We have just been focusing a lot of attention on the process of "letting go." Another important issue to consider is how we can *prevent ourselves from accumulating more unwanted and unnecessary "stuff" that keeps our light from shining*, be it feelings, people we don't enjoy, or beliefs and attitudes that don't fit.

It seems that we often talk about "saying no" when we talk about staying uncluttered in our lives. Perhaps looking at how we can more effectively say "no" could help us in this cleaning and clearing process—or at least to better keep us clean and clear longer!

My good friend Bonnie gave me a copy of a newsletter by Christiane Northrup, MD, in which she wrote a short piece about saying "no." This newsletter, by the way, is no longer published, but the information about them follows. (Dr. Christiane Northrup's *Health Wisdom for Women*, Phillips Publishing, Inc. pgs. 2–4. Her monthly hotline message is "Wisdom Wire" at 301–762–6061.)

Read on. I think you'll see how it fits with our agenda for this Project!

Rejuvenate Yourself With One Little Word—"NO!"

"Have you ever run into somebody you haven't seen in years, and you can't get over how great the person looks? Recently, I had a chance to see two colleagues who I hadn't seen in twenty years. One is a physician with several children and a hectic work schedule. It was wonderful to see that she was as youthful, bright and cheery as when I last saw her, despite dealing with managed care, and all the hassles of her profession.

"My other colleague is a musician. Now, you'd expect that she, too, would look spectacular given that her profession is teaching and making music. But that was definitely not the case! When I saw her, I couldn't believe that she was the same beautiful woman I had known in college.

"On the surface you'd expect that the surgeon would have more inherent 'stress' in her life than the musician. So why was my doctor-friend so radiant? She said, 'I'm happy. I'm doing what I like to do. If I didn't, I would change things.' This woman clearly knows how to say 'yes' to what works for her and 'no' to what doesn't. And though I can't prove it, my musician-friend probably tells an entirely different story. Her face and appearance indicated that she was making compromises in her life that did not support her health optimally. To me, she was proof of how developing a pattern of saying 'yes' when you really mean 'no' can rob you of both your health and your youthful appearance.

"Learning how and when to say 'no' to others and 'yes' to yourself is a crucial skill for creating health. And, the exciting thing about mid-life is that nature quite literally gives you another chance to live life on you own terms—to re-do yourself. This can be the key to rejuvenation because saying 'no' to the things that zap your energy will leave you time for the things that bring you fulfillment and happiness. And when you are truly doing the things that support you, you avoid the emotions of resentment and anger. As a result, you'll feel better and healthier, and have the ability to arrest the deterioration associated with aging.

Why Saying "No" Makes You Feel Guilty

"While saying 'no' seems like it would be easy, often it is very difficult because it can make you feel bad. That's because our culture conditions young girls to please others. It doesn't take a little girl long to recognize people-pleasing and self-sacrifice as a way to feel worthy. And this becomes a powerful reinforcement for you, as a woman, to continue this behavior so that you can fit in. As a result, you may often feel guilty when you get up the courage to say 'no' to others who request your time and attention.

"This is normal because women are relational creatures. We need others to love us. We are both biologically and socially programmed to get a short-term 'high' when we meet someone else's needs—even though we are not always aware of it—because society approves of us when we do this. Unfortunately, this lack of consciousness often becomes a habit that

is difficult to break. Your awareness of the long-term bad feelings that come from saying 'no' keeps you hooked on saying 'yes.' And personally, I don't know of any remedy that will prevent this emotion. However, I still recommend that you learn to say 'no' just don't be surprised if you feel bad or guilty afterwards, especially the first few times."

So there you have it, a perfect example of how we collect anger and resentment, by doing things we really don't want to do. She goes on to say that it's important that we not say "no" to everything, since that's what two-year-olds do when the are individuating from their parents. She encourages each of us to evaluate when it is the best time to say 'no' and offers these suggestions to consider as you make that determination:

- Is someone asking you to something that compromises your self-respect, self-esteem, or integrity, or somehow just doesn't feel right?
- Would fulfilling the other person's need detract from your own sense of well being?
- Does the other person's request come at a bad time so that it detracts from your own health and happiness in some way?
- Have you fallen into a pattern in which you are always doing for, or giving to, another person, but never getting anything back?

For support in how to say "no," I recommend looking into some assertiveness training.

Here are her suggestions for "When to Say Yes."

- When saying "yes" will enhance a relationship and timing is right.
- When saying "yes" will enhance your sense of well being.
- When you have reciprocity, such as when a relationship is mutually satisfying and the other person frequently does things for you.

Back to the writing . . .

III. Choose one or more healthy reasons for saying "no" and describe how *not* following that guideline has made your life more complicated. If you set aside your fears about how others might feel at first, how would saying "no" more often be helpful to you and to your inner Spirit?

IV. (As Dr. Northrup points out, the more you set boundaries by saying "no," the less likely others will be to walk on you or make unreasonable requests.)

V.   Taking action: Practice some time during this week, saying "no" in a healthy way. Experiment with how it can be useful to you. Remember that everyone will respond differently, and it will be up to you to take care of your own feelings.

VI. Before taking that *Action Step*, explore your mixed feelings. Create a dialogue, between the part of you that wants to make changes with the part of you that does **not** want to make changes—but wants to keep the peace.

VII. As you are reading this material and thinking about your life and the situations within, you are probably remembering some times when you wish you had said no, or a situation in which you did so and had a bad reaction. Pick one of those times, and write about it very briefly. Then rewrite it as you would have liked it to be. Make it an interaction that was healthy for you and for the person you were dealing with.

The purpose of writing about the original experience—and then rewriting it—is to learn about how you *want* to take your power back. Giving yourself a chance to "practice" by writing it out will help you when you want to do it in your everyday life. It can also help you learn how to deal with any guilt that may appear.

This has been an intensive session. Think of a way you can reward yourself for all the work you've done. What would be a healthy and fun reward? How do you reward yourself after cleaning? A nice bubble bath? Time out of the house? Window shopping? Give yourself some freedom to imagine a fun reward, and—if you can—***do it***!

Session 4

In this session, our focus will lead us more toward saying *"Yes."* We can learn how to say "yes" to our Spirit by using that "creative no" that was described in the Christiane Northrup article you read in Session 3. You might also look at Julia Cameron's book, **The Artist's Way** to learn about "Artist Dates" and how she recommends that you nurture yourself.

I.   Begin with the regular **Five Minute Sprint** about where you are at this time. Let yourself go, clearing your mind to be as present as you can be for the remainder of the exercises . . . Enjoy!

II.   This time as you use your **JournalCards**, turn them over so you can see the pictures. Go through them and pick the ones that fit your definition of being a person whose **Spirit** is open and receptive to growth. With those cards in hand, write your description of your **Special Spirit Self.**

III.   Go back to the exercises in Session 1 and re-read what you wrote about how you thought you might feel at the end of this process. Compare it to how you really do feel, and try to include all the ups and the downs you've experienced since Session 1.

◆ *Share, in any way that is comfortable, with your fellow group members.*

IV.   Make a list of the new actions and behaviors you hope to make part of your regular activities in life. Write yourself an **Unsent Letter**, honoring who you are, how your Authentic Self offers value to the world, and how you support her becoming more and more whole over time.

V.   Have some fun by pulling out crayons or markers and drawing a picture—in fun and full color—of your Essential Self. What colors *are* you? Know that it needn't be a form you are drawing . . . or a picture of a person, but could simple be an abstract combination of colors and movement and lines. Have fun!

VI.   In addition, or alternatively, you could begin a collage of *"Your Shining Spirit."* Use words and pictures from magazines and other places, and then glue them together on a poster board. This is another fun way to celebrate your growth and health!

VII.   *"I AM . . ."* Finish "I am . . ." In as many ways as you can. Allow yourself to repeat and don't censor! Take your **List** to 100! It will help you see *more* of who you are and all your magnificent dimensions (and may show you more that you want to release, too)!

VIII.   Finish your time on this topic, with a message from your Inner Spirit to you, your personality self. Let her speak to you through your pen, and as you open, ask for her blessing. You may want to use your non-dominant hand to speak as your Spirit Self.

How Does My Garden Grow? Expanding into My More Authentic Self!

I t is always our hope that the suggestions offered here will help you to know yourself more truly, realize and appreciate more of your gifts, be able to release blocks and disturbances that do not serve you, and grow and expand into more of who you really are!

Journaling is a unique and powerful tool with which to make many discoveries, especially with a little guidance in terms of questions asked, and people with whom you can share new realizations, if you are able to do these exercises within a group. In using a journal we each enter wherever we are in terms of our own growth, and proceed without comparing ourselves to others, to grow at our own pace. Simple and profound, and what I love so, about the process. And so you are invited to take a deep breath, open to more of yourself, and to enjoy this series of writing exercises.

The title for this project came to me as a follow up to the previous project, *"Spring Cleaning for the Spirit"*. I was interested in looking at how we continue to grow—just as we see our gardens take off during the summer months—and how, in that process we become more of who we truly are. Just as we clean up and plant seeds in the spring, we see those seedlings turn into plants, bearing fruit or flowers as we move into summer. So it is for us as human beings, that we go through our own seasonal shifts, clearing, planting, growing, and eventually harvesting from our personal life gardens. My hope is that you will be able to see more of the growth that you have already achieved, what you still want to see grow within and around you, and also to realize more of the power—fertilizer-- that you have to apply to your desires. As we open to our more authentic selves we have even more power—much like a garden that has been well weeded, well nourished and protected from contaminants. So let's get to work on our inner gardens!

Session 1

I.   This first "**Five Minute Sprint**" helps you to move from having our focus on outward or external focus, to shift into paying attention to what's going on, and how you feel inside. This is the place that seems to be harder and harder to get to as we are bombarded with more and more energy, noise and responsibilities from the outside.

II.   *JournalCards*! Now, as we move into this spiraling process of moving deeper within, it helps to pick a *JournalCard* to aid your journaling focus. You may want to just think to yourself, "what do I need to be reminded of", as you pick your card. We all, I believe, have access to all the wisdom we need, but must be reminded that we can access it. This is one method for getting in there. Let your card help stir you so that you can be directed to current life concerns or awareness's. My suggestion is to write for just about 5 or 10 minutes on what springs to mind as you write. If you remind yourself to be as honest as you can be it will help you move closer to your truth and your authentic you.

III.   So, staying with the metaphor of the garden, I want you to think about what your life garden looks like. You might even have some fun by drawing a picture to symbolize your garden. (Drawing in your journal is like journaling in that it is for your eyes only and does not have to be beautiful any more than your writing has to be grammatically correct. So draw your picture, or just begin to describe what you have going on now in your life (garden). You can use the technique called **Clustering** to help you with this task. If you draw your picture you may want to do the clustering afterward.

When you are through with your **Clustering** you have a picture of your thoughts—which engages more of your brain—which is one of the benefits of this technique. You may have a new view and additional insights that come as a result of looking at your life in this way. When you are through, it's a good idea to write a sentence or two about what you discovered in the exercise. (Some people don't like **Clustering**—creating a **List** will work, too.

I like recommending **Clustering**, especially at the beginning of a class, because it gives you a chance to pull a lot of thoughts together. As you become clearer about what you have in your life now you will get clearer about what you would like to create in your life as you grow. I hope, as you did the exercise, that you were able to see what's good in your life, as well as those areas that need a boost. As we think about making changes we need to consider what we actually control. With a highlighter, mark those areas over which you do have some control.

Do you notice the deepening that occurs in your thinking as you move from one exercise to the next? As you move more deeply within, you'll have much more clarity about yourself and what is important to you now. I find that to be so even as I put the class together.

IV. So now, how about creating a **Cluster** of the way you would *like* your life to look? Add in the things you like about what's going on in your life now, and then the changes you desire. After you are through you can again examine your ideas to see which you control and which you do not. So begin with a circle in the center of your page, this time, looking at, in a sense, how you *wish* your life garden looked. What's growing, what's been 'pulled out' of your garden? Where is the new growth . . . or the new bed that needs to be prepared? Allow yourself to *dream!* Again, when through, write just a few sentences to describe what you learned in the process.

Now you have a picture, at least for today, of what is going on in your life and what you would *like* to have going on in your life. This combination of exercises, as well as the next one, is a good one to do any time you want to reflect on where you are and where you are going. They are basic—and always useful.

Sometimes we wonder why we are where we are and seemingly unable to make greater strides in living the life we want. For those things that are out of our control we need acceptance . . . or forgiveness, and for those things that are in our control we often need courage.

V. Explore now, again with a **Cluster**, the *obstacles* that keep you from what you want or what you think you want. Most journal writers, I've noticed, already understand that *they* are responsible for their own lives. With that in mind, and remembering that no one else will see your journal, be as honest as you can be about how *you* keep yourself from what you most want. Write down *all* the obstacles you can think of that keep you from your 'perfect garden.' What keeps you from being all that you are or getting where you want to be?

VI. Now we have some basic information from which to draw during the next few weeks. As you look over your *obstacles*, see which, if any, can be easily remedied. You might want to take some time to create an **action plan** to begin to deal with one of these obstacles, even if it is just a *baby* step in that direction. The only deficit I find with journaling is that sometimes we write instead of doing . . . and many times we need to *do* in order to make our lives better. Create an *Action Step* now and write it on your calendar.

I have had a fascination with books for most of my adult life. I realized some time ago that books offered a safe non-confrontational method for me to grow and change. They, like journaling, allowed me to read and absorb what I could, all in my own way and time. Consider what books have been important to you—perhaps you have some recent favorites or perhaps you recall some that are classic for you, books that you can return to for solace and as well as direction.

VII. What I'd like to suggest is that you gather several—3 or 4—of your favorite books, together. Close your eyes and carefully pick up each one, one at a time. Notice how each feels to you—how it smells, the weight, and, if you notice, even the energy it carries, still with your eyes closed. After you have taken time with each one, pick just one of them that feels best to you right now. If you want, take a minute to write a few sentences about why this book is special to you.

VIII. After you have done that, take a moment to consider the Obstacles you described earlier. Pick one of those obstacles, and with that clearly embedded in your mind, imagine that *all* the books that you love have a collective voice. They begin to express to you as you write, how you can deal with getting more of what you want in life, and in dealing with your obstacles in particular. Write it as a script and know that the answers are all around you.

Session 2

A great workshop presenter and delightful person, Angeles Arrien, once asked the question of a group, "What did you want to do as a child, when you grew up?" In other words, in your play, what did you do, how did you play—and that will give you a clue about what it is you have come to do in your life.

For me, I remember well many days, especially in the summer, where I played school with my little friend, Marliss. We would both want to be the teacher, of course!

Think back for yourself and consider what you did as a child. Does it tell you more about your chosen profession or what you would really like to be doing?

I thought about this as I was thinking about the exercises for this project, because I'd like for us to focus on *teachers*. I guess that on some level I've always wanted to teach, to offer classes. (The question about what you did for play when you were young could be something you explore in your journal in some personal time, separate from this class.)

I think that teachers in our lives have shaped all of us, for better or worse. I know I have some *very* wonderful and special memories of teachers who essentially saved my life. Some people, as I've discovered in doing these classes, also have teachers who have been destructive to them—to their confidence or to their self-esteem. And then, there are those people or situations that become teachers in the broader sense, but are not formal teachers. These may be among the most powerful lessons we learn in our lives. So, we have all kinds of connections to teachers and learning . . . and will be exploring them in our session for this time.

I.   To begin, start with a **Five Minute Sprint**. Give yourself permission to just get your pen moving and see what wants to come out. Allow the very mundane and obvious to be expressed, if that is where you are, because we must always begin with our current state of mind.

II.   *JournalCards*. The purpose of the *JournalCards*, from my point of view, is to help you focus more clearly, deepen into your wisdom and then write from that wiser place. Because each person picks their own card, and because they will be different from day to day, you have the chance to see how the cards speak to your current reality. One time you may be struck by the word, another time the picture and another time one of the questions will be just perfect for you. Hold the cards "loosely" since they are meant to help you discover forgotten wisdom within, and not meant to tell you anything in particular.

Let your card or cards today help you simply to deepen, to be more honest with yourself, to perhaps risk writing about something that has been on the edge of your consciousness but until now not ready to be put into words. However you do this, be gentle with yourself, and be respectful of your particular journey. There is no right way to do it, this journal writing, so you can feel at ease that *your way is just right for you.* It's all part of the wonderful personal acceptance that can come as you create a deeper relationship with your Journal.

So, here we are now ready to explore more of our inner wisdom about how we learn and what we have learned. Again, I like to use a "wide brush" kind of exercise so you can have a better picture of your history of learning. To do that we'll use Progoff's exercise called "**Steppingstones.**"

III.   Begin with "I was born . . ." as the first **Steppingstone**. Then proceed, just as they emerge in your mind, writing down a total of only 8 to 12 more learning steps that have made a significant mark on your life. Continue to list, as they occur to you, the rest of your learning **Steppingstones**.

When we look at our learning history, we discover just how many varieties of experiences we have had. I have a tendency, personally, to 'soften' my history so nothing seems so bad in my memory. While there's nothing wrong with that, I think it can keep me (at times) from really digging in to an issue, and keeps me from being as authentic as I might be. For that reason, I've decided to offer you the next exercise as a way to look at both sides of the learning process—the pleasant with the difficult. I call it "***Looking at the MONSTERS and the MENTORS our lives.***"

IV.   Why not begin just by writing, again for about **five minutes**, about what comes up for you as you think of those words—*monsters* and *mentors*. Who are they now, who were they when you were young? How do you relate to those words? Please don't spend time thinking first, but just jump in—that is one way that the power of journaling shows itself as you just open to see what comes out.

Remember as you write about past and present monsters and mentors that this is for your eyes only. Take some risks as you write and say some things that haven't been said before. This is part of the releasing benefit of your journal. My belief is that we are letting go of "emotional constipation" as we write, cleaning our bodies and souls from unnecessary garbage.

◆ *When we do this exercise in my face-to-face groups there are almost always lots of surprised people who talked with some passion about the monsters in their lives. See what comes up for you and decide whether you would like to share some with a larger group.*

Choose now one of those *Monsters* or *Mentors* to describe in greater detail. Which, as you think about which you want to explore, do you think will be of greater value to you now? As you are *learning* while you write to and about yourself, you have the power to choose your focus. Which is most important to you now? Do you need release or do you need affirmation?

V. Before you begin this description you may want to make short lists of the monsters and mentors in your life. Pick one that seems important to you today. (You can always write about others later.) See if there is one particular scene that you can picture in your mind, to help you with the focus of this description. Close your eyes briefly and take a deep breath. Imagine that scene, even feeling yourself stepping (safely) back into it and knowing that JUST the right descriptive words will flow from your pen as you jump in and begin.

◈ *Again, decide if this is something you want to share with the group.*

VI. So now, how about tuning in to one of your Mentors? You have a short list, so, based on what is going on in your life right now, pick one, or create an idealized one, and invite them to come to your assistance now. Let them know your concerns, your desires and your affection and respect for them. You may do it in the form of an **Unsent Letter**.

VII. Now that you are tuned in to that special Mentor, I now invite you to begin a **Dialogue** with her/him. Ask her/him to aid you in your current challenges, your current area of growth, and to help you understand what your present is all about, how best to move forward.

VIII. Let this guide of yours help you know more about being fully yourself, and acknowledge you for the work you are doing to get to your authentic self. Breathe deeply before beginning and remind yourself to open, open, open to the greater wisdom that is available to you.

IX. What stirs? Note how you feel, what you are led to do or to plan for your life enhancement. Enjoy your self-discovery.

X. As an additional 'fun' exercise, I'd suggest that you pick one current challenge or area of growth to focus upon. Imagine that one of your mentors, or one you would like to know but only admire, is picking your next three *JournalCards*. They are helping YOU select just the right cards to help you move forward. You will pick three cards:

- to describe the current challenge in your life
- to describe some hint about an *Action Step* you can take
- to describe the new situation that will come as you do take action

◈ *Consider sharing with the group what your three cards and how they impacted you! How do you see them as useful as you consider "How Does My Garden Grow?" Note, too, what (if any) increased intimacy you have achieved within yourself as you move through these exercises.*

Session 3

I hope that you are all enjoying your lives, and that you feel your growth just as you see the plants around you growing.

There are so many different things we can talk about in this broad question of how do we learn and grow.

One of the assumptions that I make in guiding these sessions is that each of us is still striving toward something in our lives. It could be that we are very happy in many ways, but there is always something, I believe, that can be enhanced. Even if I were just working on gratitude, my desire would be to be more deeply grateful for more.

By saying that I'm setting the stage for more of what we will focus on in these exercises. I picked up a book recently by Herbert Benson, M.D. Some of you may remember him as the Harvard doctor who developed the **Relaxation Response,** which has been such an important concept in mind/body healing. His new book is called **The Break-Out Principle**. I was drawn to it by the additional description, which says, "How to activate the natural trigger that maximizes creativity, athletic performance, productivity, and personal well-being." Doesn't that sound intriguing to you? It was interesting to me because I had scribbled myself a note while putting this class together about adding "relax and release" as an important concept I wanted to cover. I offer you some excerpts from this book so you can see what I am talking about, and you may just be led to go buy the book for yourselves!

> *"So what exactly is the Breakout Principle?"* In a nutshell, here is our basic working definition:
>
> The Breakout Principle refers to a powerful mind-body impulse that severs prior mental patterns and—even in times of great stress or emotional trauma—opens an inner door to a host of personal benefits, including greater mental activity, enhanced creativity, increased job productivity, maximal athletic performance and spiritual development."

Clearly, the definition suggests that there is an inner switch that can be turned on and will help to cut ties to negative thinking patterns and help to move into a transformational state.

Here are the five stages of the Breakout Principle, which I will take from his book with some additional explanation as well. I think you will all identify with this to some extent—I know I did—and what is most interesting to me is that he is offering scientific backup for all these claims. Learning is visible on so many levels, all enhancing our personal learning so well.

"Principle #1: A Breakout begins with your natural power to maximize health, mental ability, and physical performance."

"Before a self-improvement program can work effectively, significant emotional roadblocks—such as deep phobias, debilitating stress, or other emotional traumas—must first be swept away . . .."

"Sometimes, these inner obstacles are so serious that they must be dealt with professionally, either through counseling or medications. But in many cases, interfering emotional barriers can be minimized or eliminated automatically through the Breakout mechanism. The reason for this is that every Breakout is rooted in our innate, self-healing, stress-reducing biological and bio-chemical package, which inspired the great Greek physician Hippocrates to extol the natural restorative abilities of the human body . . . . ."

" . . . you have been born with an array of biological triggers that you can "pull" to activate life-changing Breakouts." (p. 14/15)

"Principle #2: The same mind-body mechanism operates in every Breakout trigger. "

"The fundamental mechanism for activating every Breakout can be stated rather simply:

To trigger a Breakout, you must sever completely your previous train of thoughts and emotions.

This decisive disruption of prior mental patterns will enable you to shift your focus into new and more productive directions. Achieving such a break in your old mental tapes in an absolute prerequisite if you hope to experience dramatic new spiritual insights, creative breakthroughs, or leaps to new heights of professional or athletic achievement." (p. 16)

"Principle #3: As a Breakout begins, your body and mind move through a series of distinct, identifiable stages."

"Typically, the Breakout Principle encompasses an inner process that consists of four distinct stages:

The process begins with a hard mental or physical struggle.

The second stage involves pulling the breakout trigger.

The third stage in the Breakout process is the Breakout proper, coupled with a peak experience.

Finally, the Breakout cycle finishes with a fourth stage, which involves returning to a "new-normal" state—including ongoing improved performance and mind-body patterns." (p. 19)

"Principle #4: Activating the trigger appears to cause your body to release puffs of nitric oxide—a response that counters stress hormones that can impede a Breakout."

"The overall calming of the mind and body—which I identified in scientific studies almost three decades ago as the relaxation response—is also associated with a number of stress reducing events . . . These include reduced blood pressure, lower heart rate, and an overall lowering of the metabolism." (p. 21)

" Principle #5: A 'peak experience' often follows a Breakout."

" . . . Maslow argued that the greatest personal creativity, well being, and philosophical understanding became possible when a person moved up to the highest, self-actualization level. Furthermore, at the level of self-actualization, the individual was more likely to have a 'peak experience,' characterized by great insight, freedom from fear and anxiety, and a sense of being unified with an infinite or eternal dimension of reality." (p. 22)

The "trigger" that Benson talks about in this process can be one of a great number of activities. His book creates an extensive list of which I'll just share a few: prayer, meditation, running, walking, looking at a work of art, listening to music, taking a shower, etc.

Pretty much anything that helps you "***shift***" into a new space can be a trigger. Journaling, too, can be a trigger, if you leave your "issue" behind, and write about something completely different and unrelated to the problem you are facing at the time.

I.   We'll come back to look at this information as we move along with our journaling exercises. For now you can begin, as usual, with writing for about five minutes. Perhaps you can give yourself permission to turn on some music and breathe quietly for about five minutes before you even begin to write. Just sitting quietly and letting your mind empty would be another way to move gently into these exercises. Enjoy the process.

II.   *JournalCards*. As you pick one card at a time, ask to be reminded of something that will help you in your learning and growing process. Write for five or ten minutes about those cards that you pull.

As part of following the guidelines in the Breakout Principle, lets take some time to shift gears. What would you think of spending some time in just writing about happy times? So often my counselor self wants to "work" on issues rather than just enjoying what IS, so in THIS class we will take some time to enjoy our happiness, past and present.

So, as we explore happy days, how would you rate yourself in terms of how much time you spend being happy? On a scale of one to ten, one being not at all, and ten being almost all the time, where are you—on average, of course. Start with looking at the last week, then the last month, then the last year and then your life, applying the one to ten scale for each.

III.   After you've done that, writing as fast as you can, make a **List**—at least to 50—of those things that make you happy. Write quickly and it's okay to repeat!

IV.   Pick one of those happy times and play with it a little. Begin by describing in detail just what was going on, and how you knew you were happy. After writing that initial description try this: Pick up your pen in your *non-dominant hand*, and let your inner child tell you what *she* thinks is really, really fun. Create a dialogue with her if you like, exploring *her* fun and how she might help you to have even more fun.

V.   What stirs? What comes up for you as you move through these exercises? Are there questions you have you would like to ask the group? Are there insights you have that you would like to share? Take about five minutes to process your thoughts about all this on paper.

Relaxing and releasing seems to be the biggest factor, the "trigger," in the Breakout Principle. How are you at taking charge of your life in that way? It seems to me that many of us know how to be busy, to 'work' on our issues in a serious way, but I wonder how well we do with taking time to relax and release? It's something I need more conscious awareness of myself . . . and so we all get to do this exercise!

VI.   For this exercise I'd like to take you back to **Lists** . . . and ask that you make a list to 100, allowing yourself to repeat, of all the ways you can think of that you relax and release tension, fear, doubt, anger. 100 seems like a lot, but really—if you write quickly and allow yourself to repeat—you will find your list to be very revealing. When done you can count the number of most repeated activities and see that it is a percentage of your total 100. For instance, if you say "take a bath" six times, then 6% of your attitudes about relaxing and releasing include taking a bath, I do believe, and the book ***The Break-out Principle*** backs it up, that we need to know how to relax and release—surrender—in order to continue to grow to our greatest heights.

VII. To wrap up this session's exercises I'd like to suggest to you an **Alphapoem**. It's a simple and often enlightening way to write in a shorthand kind of way about our beliefs about a given topic. In this case I'd suggest you choose whichever topic feels most vivid or juicy to you. For instance, you may find that you really connected with the whole idea of happiness and want to do your poem about that—or you may want to look at the idea of relaxation and letting go as your theme. Pick whichever fits best for you.

I know some people have spoken about being intimidated with the idea of a poem, only then to discover what fun they can be. So let yourself experiment and remember that, like drawing and writing about tender subjects, it's for your eyes only. You may be surprised and want to share it, eventually!

VIII. I know, I promised that the exercise above was the last one in this Session, but I suddenly feel compelled to return to my "old faithful," which is to create an *Action Step* in your life that will help you to take some or all of the insight gained in this session and implement it into your life.

◆ *With your group: Talk about goofy and fun things that you are doing in your summer activities. Especially try sharing those things that make no sense, have no reason behind them, but at the same time leave you feeling fresh and alive!!*

Session 4

Ultimately, I believe that we are all seeking inner peace. Growing is an ongoing process that follows cycles like the seasons of the year. Growing into our most authentic selves is also a cyclical deepening process that, I believe, is characterized, by more and more time spent in an attitude of peace. As we get wiser our times of peace can be extended . . . and this, I think, is the greatest gift we can offer to the world. As each of us reaches more inner peace we can influence, one at a time, the greater peace.

Thich Nhat Hanh is a spiritual teacher who teaches mindfulness as a way of impacting not only our lives but also the world. I'm including two brief essays from his book, **Peace is Every Step,** for you to enjoy. I offer thanks to his publishing company as we share these articles here.

"Interbeing"

"If you are a poet, you will see clearly that there is a cloud floating in this sheet of paper. Without a cloud, there will be no rain; without rain, the trees cannot grow; and without trees, we cannot make paper. The cloud is essential for the paper to exist. If we can say that the cloud and the paper inter-are. "Interbeing" is a word that is not in the dictionary yet, but if we combine the prefix "inter-" with the verb "to be," we have a new very, inter-be.

If we look into this sheet of paper even more deeply, we can see the sunshine in it. Without sunshine, the forest cannot grow. In fact, nothing can grow without sunshine. And so, we know that the sunshine is also in this sheet of paper. The paper and the sunshine inter-are. And if we continue to look, we can see the logger who cut the tree and brought it to the mill to be transformed into paper. And we see wheat. We know that the logger cannot exist without his daily bread, and therefore the wheat that became his bread is also in this sheet of paper. The logger's father and mother are in it too. When we look in this way, we see that without all of these things, this sheet of paper cannot exist.

Looking even more deeply, we can see ourselves in this sheet of paper, it is part of our perception. Your mind is in here and mine is also. So we can say that everything is in here with this sheet of paper. We cannot point out one thing that is not here—time, space, the earth, the rain, the minerals in the soil, the sunshine, the cloud, the river, the heat. Everything co-exists with this sheet of paper. That is why I think the word inter-be should be in the dictionary. "To be" is to inter-be. We cannot just be by ourselves alone. We have to inter-be with every other thing. This sheet of paper is because everything else is.

Suppose we try to return one of the elements to its source. Suppose we return the sunshine to the sun. Do you think that this sheet of paper will be possible? No, without sunshine nothing can be. And if we return the

> *logger to his mother, then we have no sheet of paper either. The fact is that this sheet of paper is made up only of "non-paper" elements. And if we return these non-paper elements their sources, then there can be no paper at all. Without non-paper element, like mind, logger, sunshine and so on, there will be no paper. As thin as this sheet of paper is, it contains everything in the universe in it." (p 95/96)*

I appreciate this article because it reminds me that we are all connected—that indeed, everything is connected. He does so in a very practical way, and in a non-judgmental way. I want to add another of his pieces from this book, since it speaks about being tuned in to our world—even though the book was published in 1991. I'll let you draw your own conclusions from it.

"Waging Peace"

> *"If the earth were your body, you would be able to feel the many areas where it is suffering. War, political and economic oppression, famine, and pollution wreak havoc in so many places. Every day, children are becoming blind from malnutrition, their hands searching hopelessly through mounds of trash for a few ounces of food. Adults are dying slowly in prisons for trying to oppose violence. Rivers are dying, and the air is becoming more and more difficult to breathe. Although the two great super-powers are becoming a little friendlier, they still have enough nuclear weapons to destroy the Earth dozens of times.*
>
> *Many people are aware of the world's suffering; their hearts are filled with compassion. They know what needs to be done, and they engage in political, social, and environmental work to try to change things. But after a period of intense involvement they may become discouraged if they lack the strength needed to sustain a life of action. Real strength is not in power, money or weapons, but in deep, inner peace.*
>
> *Practicing mindfulness in each moment of our daily lives, we can cultivate our own peace. With clarity, determination, and patience—the fruits of meditation—we can sustain a life of action and be real instruments of peace. I have seen this peace in people of various religious and cultural backgrounds who spend their time and energy protecting the weak, struggling for social justice, lessening the disparity between rich and poor, stopping the arms race, fighting against discrimination, and watering the trees of love and understanding throughout the world." (p. 99/100)*

For me, I feel motivated to spend more time in meditation/prayer, to seek more peace——and at the same time, it helps me in the Breakout Principle as well. Hope this adds to your learning, too.

I.   Having taken this time to read before starting our exercises, you may have already slowed your breathing and moved into that "inner space." If you have it will be even easier for you to take this initial **Five Minute Sprint** to take you more deeply within. As usual, allow this time to be a freeing time when you can let go of surface concerns so that you will be freer to open to your present moment and your present wisdom. Write for just about five minutes.

II. As you continue this weekly pattern you will see that it may be a process that you find useful whenever you journal, and using these initial exercises may help you deepen into your very own "magic." You can ask to be reminded of what is of greatest importance to you, as you draw your cards, or you can ask for help in being directed to greater peace. You will choose, but do take the time to breathe deeply again, pick a card with intent, and then allow pen . . . and begin to write about your beliefs and attitudes about peace . . . and how it impacts your life and growth.

III. If you are like me, when you delve into the topic of finding more peace you may find yourself short on answers, or at least frustrated by all the dissenters to peace that are in your life/world. For that reason I'd like to suggest next that you take some time—ten minutes or so, to write prayerfully, an invitation for more peace to enter where it is now missing, or lacking. As you write, experiment with softening your mind and heart, forgiving those (as I am now as I write) who frustrate you, and asking for guidance and direction. Ask for help in bringing more peace and love into your life.

IV. I'd like, now to suggest a wonderful exercise that can help you move into more of your personal depth and more of your inner peace. It is using the **Alphapoem** that we used in the last class, but with a twist. In this can you will only use ten letters to begin a poem. Go to the last exercise you wrote . . . and read through it, underlining strong, meaningful and powerful phrases. Pick one of those phrases that help you to grasp the meaning of peace for you—and use that phrase as the title for your first "ten letter" **Alphapoem**. So, begin with the first letter of your first name and write them vertically down the left side of your page. For example, I would start with S and then write ten more letters . . . and when I hit Z would start again with A. Ten letters from S would be B. Then write the phrase you have chosen as your title and begin your poem.

- When you have finished, remembering to just let the words flow and not be concerned about making it perfect. Read over your poem. Pick out the most powerful line, the most forward moving line, and make THAT the title for another ten-letter poem. Pick up where you left off, so I would begin with the letter C and write it vertically down my page until I got to L.

- As you use a line from the first poem to fuel your ideas for the second one, you'll go through the same process when finished with it. Read it over and pick the juiciest line and make that the title for your third poem. Again, pick up where you left off in the letters, M, for me, and write ten more letters.

When you are done with this **"Series of Three"** exercise you will have dipped into more interesting inner resources.

V.   So, having done that exploration, take some time now, with heart and mind opened as wide as you can, to respond to what you have written. What does all this mean to you? How does it affect your daily life? What are the *Action Steps* you can now create to help you enter in to more peace every day? I encourage you, as I have throughout this book, to dig in deeply, open to yourself, risk uncovering more of what has kept you from peace, and gently forgive, accept, honor and release whenever possible. This is all part of "minding the garden" of our lives.

VI.   Back to the garden! I suggest that you again—or for the first time— take some time to draw a picture of your garden. Pull out some crayons or markers and let yourself peacefully play as you imagine what you would plant where. Remember that it is just for you so it doesn't have to be a work of art, but rather just the opportunity to be quietly with yourself, and imagining this garden, can bring you into a wonderful relaxed and refreshed place. (I recently bought a book of "mandalas" for people in my retreats to color. Their intent is to create a peaceful space just by focusing on color and design—much like another Breakout trigger.) Create an abstract garden! Enjoy your own heavenly view of what you would put there. Or, imagine it as your "secret garden" and, if you haven't read the book, I heartily encourage you to do so!

VII.   In my face-to-face journal classes we often do guided imagery, where I speak and people close their eyes to imagine. It is a great tool for dipping in more deeply to our inner 'magic'. In this case we're going to try something a little different. Instead of 'listening' to someone else I want to try another experiment. What I'm hoping to create is an opportunity for you to 'hear' the wisdom that now comes to you from your garden (symbolic, of course, for your lives). You could take some time to look at the drawing you've made of your thriving garden, you could look at an actual garden you have tended, you could pull out pictures from a magazine, or you could just close your eyes and see this thriving and lush garden in your minds eye. Be sure to allow enough time to really relax into this. Take time to be with your garden . . . and listen then, for what it has to say to you about its beauty and abundance, and about what it still needs, how it is doing in growth, and what, if anything, that means for you. So you are "anthropomorphizing" your garden (making it human) and giving it a voice. Listen for the wonderful, earthy wisdom it has for you . . . and listen for any directions it has for you as you move ahead. When ready, pick up your pen . . . and allow your garden to 'speak' to you.

I hope you will have fun with this experiment, as with others offered in this project and throughout the book. I hope, too, that more peace is available to you, and that all of us, working together, can produce an enormous impact on peace in the world.

Project Nine

Seasons, Transitions and Me!

Our topic this month comes from the changing seasons we are encountering, but also with the knowing that we are ALWAYS going through change and transition, and are in need of support for that process.

The shift into each new season seems to be a big one, bigger than even the New Year for some of us drenched in the educational system. At the same time, each season has its "triggers," either positive or negative, and we collect them throughout our lives. As we move toward fall, even those of us in the Sun Belt think about school, fall colors, upcoming holidays, as well as whatever personal shifts may be going on. (Know that you can enjoy these sessions in any season.)

Certainly these shifts and changes are all about *life!* Many try to avoid change, but it is always with us, and would be easier to manage and cope with, perhaps, as we understand it better and learn to accept what change brings.

One of the books I have used in counseling for many years is called ***Transitions; Making Sense of Life's Change***s, by William Bridges. It offers a simple model for understanding the stages of transition. Many, myself included, have found it comforting and relieving as we plug the model into our own lives and see what is going on and that we have been through this same process over and over in our lives. Here is the basis of the model. Read over it . . . and then we will begin our writing!

Bridges explains that while *change* is the experience we have in real time, such as moving, or changing jobs, or seasons, it is *transition* that he uses to describe the internal or psychological response to that change. While a change may occur in a day, the transition may last for months, depending upon the intensity of the shift.

The transition process is broken into three stages:

- **Endings.** All transitions begin with an ending——something is being given up. Even if the change is perceived as positive the ending brings up loss. There are four elements of endings: disengagement; disenchantment; disorientation; dis-identification.
- **Neutral Zone.** An uncomfortable time when the old way of being no longer fits, and the new way is not yet together. A time of emptiness, and many emotions. More grief comes up as endings get worked through. This time can create a sense of vulnerability that we react to in different ways. This is a time when communication, inside and out, is very important.
- **New beginnings.** The new form emerges in its own time and own way, much as a flower that blooms according to its own timetable. An important element in supporting this unfolding is by taking a look at the four P's; the purpose, a picture, the plan, and a part to play. When the new beginning takes hold a person feels; re-engaged, re-enchanted, reoriented, and re-identified.

Rarely do we go through transitions in all parts of our lives at the same time, so we can emphasize those things that remain the same while other shifts occur. The more changes that are going on in many aspects of our lives, the longer it takes to adapt and adjust to the transition.

Think about changes going on for you, the simple ones and the more complex. Breathe in, knowing that you have done this already, hundreds or thousands of times. There is always a step into the unknown . . . and that is where we feel most vulnerable. Hopefully the exercises this month will help you get more comfort with this whole process and with your deeper nature that remains stable throughout.

Session 1

I. As always, begin your writing time—after you take a deep breath and clear some space and time for yourself—with where you are. Just date your page and begin to write, let your pen take you where it needs to go. *Write for just five minutes*, with no worry about being profound or enlightened, but rather let yourself make the shift from external focus to inner awareness. You will find that you feel more *present* and more grounded as you write this first "warm-up" piece of your journal writing.

II.   After you write for five minutes in the above exercise, you will be in a better space—more aware and focused, to now pick a ***JournalCard***. Respond as you choose, not feeling compelled to answer all the questions, but rather allowing the cards just to guide you into deeper and richer parts of yourself and your life. You may want to ask yourself, "What do I need to be aware of in terms of transitions in my life?" You are welcome to pick more than one card, and let each successive card deepen your awareness. See how they fit together to give you an even more complete view of your life in the now.

◆ *Feel free to share the cards you picked and how they did or didn't fit, with the rest of the group.*

III.   Think about these different aspects of your life: Health, Work, Relationships, Family, Aging, Education/Growth, Play—and whatever other parts stand out for you as you look more closely at your life. Where are changes occurring in these diverse areas? Make a **List** of them. Then go through your list and mark each one on a scale of 1–10, with *one* being not important and *ten* being very important with respect to how they are impacting your life. Then, take a look at the changes that are occurring and see if you can apply a loose percentage, like 25% or 5% of my life may be in transition and that leaves how much stable?

◆ *You may want to note how you feel after you have written this exercise, noting new discoveries or awarenesses. It's also a good time to share bits of this with your larger group.*

IV.   Now that you see more clearly where you are dealing with change, give yourself a chance to look at those parts of your life that are stable, solid and supportive. Create a **Cluster** of those things that are essentially stable in your life and include everything you can think of.

V.   When you are finished with your **Cluster**, write a few sentences about your experience, what became clear to you and any surprises you may have discovered in doing this exercise.

VI.   Say goodbye. What have you discovered, if anything, as you have written so far, that you need to release and let go of in this transition? How well do you say goodbye? Now is a good time to formalize the changes you are going through, saying goodbye to those parts now gone, and leaving room for what is yet to come. You can use the technique of an **Unsent Letter** to accomplish this task. Include everything you can think of that needs to be released, writing more than one letter if necessary. Observe your feelings as you proceed, and include that awareness in your journal.

VII.   As we wrap up this session we'll use a guided meditation to enable the spiraling process. Take a deep breath, listen or read along as you simply follow along with these words:

✦ Meditation ✦

So get yourself into a comfortable position, breathing gently to release accumulated tensions. Give yourself time to settle in, taking with you your awareness of the shifts and changes going on within and around you now. . . . Breathe in more deeply now, letting go even more of distractions and disturbances. . . . .noting that for now . . . everything. . . . is just as you need it to be. . . . All is well. . . . no need for anxiety. . . . . As you settle deeper and deeper inside yourself. . . . .you feel lighter and lighter. . . . You imagine turning your attention inward . . . moving toward that place within that is your connection to infinite wisdom. . . . You find yourself being drawn in, closer and closer, to this area of great light . . . . . . It feels safe, warm, strengthening and powerful . . . . You soak up the energies of this space. . . . knowing that others in your group will be doing the very same thing. . . . . You feel a depth and knowing that is rich, vibrant and deeply grounding. . . . . As you move further into your place of wisdom you may allow yourself to imagine that you are encountering your wise person within. As you meet that person you feel further enriched and enlivened. Questions that you may have become more vivid as your wise person offers answers to you . . . either in words, gestures, symbols, or even in song. . . . . You stay in this space, noting the stable feelings you have in this space. . . . And bring all of this with you . . . as you slowly bring your awareness back, feeling your feet on the floor and readying yourself to pick up your pen. Now, take a deep and gentle breath, bring all of these new awarenesses with you. Pick up you pen and let it flow with the gifts received as you visited with your own inner wisdom. . . . . Enjoy.

✦

Session 2

I.   As always, begin your timed writing (**Five Minute Sprint**) where you are. If you want to vary this experience a little you could turn on some special music, and let that carry you more deeply within. Since this piece of writing is just to get you to "shift gears" you could use it as a place to experiment with letting go of your critic. Try writing without capitalization or punctuation—like many do on email. This could let you just think about what you are feeling and not focusing on any level of grammar.

II.   Deepening with *JournalCards*. As you continue to look at the changes going on in your life you can let your cards guide you further down the road of awareness. Try picking three cards as you sort through the set of cards, **picture side up**. Choose the words or pictures that "grab" you as you look through them. Then take five or so minutes to react to your choices.

III.   Since *change* involves so much disruption, it can be very useful to clear out old and unwanted thoughts and feelings from the past. It could be called letting go of Unfinished Business. One way to address that is by using the **"Steppingstones"** technique to help give you perspective about your life. List those important 'change' experiences now.

When you read over your list of important life changes you'll see that some of the steps will give you a feeling of a "charge" or "yuck" or "whoppee" as you read them. Those are indicators of "unfinished business." What you can do next then, is pick one of those topics that you know you are reacting strongly to, and let *that* be the title for another 10 minute write. Give yourself time to release more of your unfinished business—and see if there are *Action Steps* that would help you clean it up even more.

IV.   Now, pick another bit of unfinished business, and again write for about 10 minutes on another **Steppingstone**. Let it go. These could also be written as an **Unsent Letter** to help you further let go of *history that needs to be in the past.* If there are more bits of Unfinished Business to release take time to do so, or set a date to write again in the near future.

V.   As you review those two pieces of writing consider how it helped you to let go. Resolve to write about *more* pieces of unfinished business, understanding that often it takes a while to let go of it completely.

VI.   In my training for Gestalt Therapy one of the things we did as we finished groups was to share "Appreciations, Resentments and Regrets." As you look at all that has gone on in your life, as well as what is going on now, look at it all in terms of these three words.

Make three columns, with one of these words in each. Then, honestly review all your feelings about the shifts gong on in your life. The goal behind this is to not carry any more baggage into the "new beginning." This is just more cleaning up of old stuff that is better left behind.

VII.   Now refocus on those things (from last session's exercises) that remain stable in your life. Offer a prayer of gratitude to those things/people/parts of your life, that help you to stay grounded and centered in the midst of change. Write for at least five minutes.

VIII.   To lighten up a little try this exercise suggested by a friend: review old recipes. What stays the same, what changes, and what does that tell you about you and your life.

Session 3

As we move into another session, take a few minutes to just stop and take a breath. Enjoy a moment of not pushing yourself. If you have the time, wander through your journal for a bit. Flip through some back pages, remembering how even difficult things were achieved.

I.   Okay, now take about five minutes to create that "shift" into inner awareness. Let you pen show you the way as you simply go with whatever thoughts or feelings come to mind. Write without concern for making sense, "getting somewhere," or staying focused. Let it simply help you come to the present with all your disparate thoughts.

II.   *JournalCards.* Pick one to help you with a little more focus. See what comes up, how it stirs up your view of your current life. Then write away! I suggest five minutes, but you decide how much time is best for you.

III.   Describe in detail now, what you define as your greatest current challenge. If you have already written about it, do it again, with even more detail and more honesty. Be patient with yourself as you describe this time in your life including your feelings about what you are encountering. No challenge? Is that a problem too? Explore.

(There have been times in my life when 'no challenge' made my life seem empty—another kind of challenge, so don't overlook something like that for yourself.)

IV. Now, to continue with that theme, you'll have a chance to use the ***JournalCards*** to take you into a wider view of this "current challenge." As you choose your ***JournalCards***, be aware of the order that you pick them and ask, before you begin, that just the cards you need to see be made available to you. You will choose six different cards, each offering you a different perspective on your challenge. Don't hold too tightly to the questions on the cards . . . but let them gently guide you to new clarity and new points of view. Each card, in order, represents:

1. Something that no longer needs so much of your attention (may be some aspect that has been integrated into your life);
2. The "right now" moment in your life in some way;
3. An *Action Step* you would benefit from taking;
4. The newly evolved situation after you take that action;
5. Something that is coming to be in your future; and
6. Magic Card!!! Gives you wide perspective and special insight.

Take time to explore this series of cards and what it has to say to you about your transition and your current challenge.

7. Create a **Dialogue**. Do you still feel some conflict or lack of clarity in regard to your transition or challenge? For this exercise try creating a **Dialogue** between your conflicted parts. If you have a part of you that wants to move on and another that wants things to remain the same, let them talk together about their feelings. What is important in any **Dialogue** is that you have clarity about each side of the conflict or concern. Perhaps you even have an issue with another person—that makes a **Dialogue** much clearer and easier to understand. ***Pick two opposing forces in your life right now and begin your Dialogue***. Start with a question or a statement to the other party, and then respond as the other part. Though it may feel awkward initially, this is a powerful technique. As you practice it here you'll begin to realize how you might use it in other conflicted situations.

8. Now, using the technique called **Perspective**, imagine that you have moved through this time of change and transition and are

now looking back. Imagine that it is just one year from today, and you are reflecting on your life now and how you resolved your challenge and moved ahead. Enjoy this process—and open to use some imagination and intuition about the positive changes that lie before you. Date your page as though it is a year from today . . . and begin a journal entry about looking back....

Session 4

I. Once again, begin where you are each time you sit down to journal—meaning take five minutes to just write about whatever comes to mind. As you do that you will release tension, dump unnecessary thoughts and feel yourself grounded, connected and once again clearer about yourself and your desires. As you continue into your journal exercises you will also find you have more access to your wisdom . . . and of course, your "magic." So begin now, writing for just five minutes about how you feel or what you notice.

I hope you are experimenting with different ways to use your *JournalCards* . . . like drawing more than one at a time, using different cards to give you awareness about two sides of a conflict, or as a way to get a view of how you want things in the future. You can use these cards in a variety of ways—even as a discussion tool with family members.

II. For today, draw three cards, all with the intention of asking yourself to pick cards that will help you to get more in touch with your strengths, your gifts. See what shows up. If you don't want to use them that way just use them in the more straight forward way of letting them guide you to deeper aspects of your life as you follow suggestions offered on the card.

III. For the next exercise, I ask you to quickly review your work to date. Begin to let your conscious mind and unconscious mind work together to literally "spell out" how you see yourself in you current journey. Choose the technique called "**Alphapoem.**" Remember? Write the letters of the alphabet down the left hand side of a journal page. Then let each letter of the alphabet guide you by becoming the first letter of the first word of each line of your (non-rhyming!) poem.

IV. As you quickly write your poem about a topic that has some "juice" for you, tap into the surprising parts of yourself simply by following the friendly alphabet. Shifts and changed attitudes can be another delightful surprise as you read over your new poem. Before you begin your **Alphapoem**, pick your title clearly. Let it come from the work you have done to date, or just call it **"My Current Journey."**

◈ *I hope that you enjoyed the experience of writing your Alphapoem . . . and consider whether you would like to share it, or parts of it, with your group.*

    V.   For your next exercise, write a kind of prayer, to whatever you believe in, asking for more help as you move through your current changes, and ask in particular for more opening, more clarity and more direction. (*This may begin to sound like a personal guided meditation, so consider taping it so you can hear it in your own voice—as another way to experience more of your personal power.*) You could ask for messages, for your unconscious to make conscious some important information that will help you open your heart to yourself and others. You will find your own words to ask as it fits for you. Try finding a few moments of silence before writing. Move into more quietness and deeper trust of the forces available to you. When you feel ready, pick up your pen and let it take you where you need to go, to deeper places and higher desires. Let your censors be at rest as you flow and feel the joy of open expression. Let your own divinely inspired voice speak to you.

   VI.   You may want to take some time to reflect upon that experience and make notes in your journal about how it felt and what came up for you as you did it.

  VII.   Now is a good time to review the material you have covered over the last month. See where you began, what you encountered, and where you are now with your transitional challenges. If you want you can highlight parts of your journal that now stand out as key to your growth. You could even write **Steppingstones** again, noting changes and affirming your growth and your personal power. Write questions that still linger that will carry you into even more of your journal magic.

◈ *Would you be comfortable in sharing accomplishments, new awareness's, interesting insights, or stubborn areas of stuck-ness with your group? The more we learn and accept about the process of growth and change the more it will help us all so your experience could be a powerful gift to another.*

A Fresh Start—
Reflect, Release and Recreate

The beginning of a new calendar year or a new season always seems like an invitation to take another look at where we are, what we're doing, and what we want to change.

Of course it's important to remember that our new beginnings can come in any moment—they *do* come in every moment, so we are always free to start again. I say that partly to remind you to keep these exercises so you can use them again in the future when you want to review an aspect of your life again, and partly because you may, indeed, be using these mid-year.

Journal writing is a powerful tool for each of us to use to get more in touch with ourselves and to take time to listen to our soul's message. I've begun to talk about this as "therapeutic writing" since we are not just journaling about our daily lives, but actually "working" on ourselves in a healing way, as we participate in these exercises. This writing is therapeutic as we physically do the writing and feel our pen on the page, in what we discover about ourselves as we release thoughts and feelings, and as we begin to rediscover and redefine who we are in each moment. As you may gather from reading this . . . I am very passionate about the benefits of this therapeutic writing!

Session 1

Begin in the *now!* Observe yourself in this moment and let your pen spill out what you want to be said. Do not worry about how you are writing or even what you are saying, but just get your pen moving. Breathe deeply as you enter in to this writing, and as you make the shift from focus on your external life circumstances to paying attention to your inner experience. You may offer a silent request for help as you do this, as you listen to yourself and your wishes. Write for about **five minutes** just to get warmed up and to make that shift into hearing your own inner workings.

Here are a few quotes from ***Stillness Speaks*** by Eckhart Tolle:

> *"When you lose touch with inner stillness, you lose touch with yourself. When you lose touch with yourself, you lose yourself in the world."*
> *"Your innermost sense of self, of who you are, is inseparable from stillness. This is the I Am that is deeper than name and form."*

So, breathe into that as you prepare to pick some ***JournalCards*** to help you with moving more deeply into your *now.*

Picking your ***JournalCards***---always begin with an intention of picking just the right cards for this time, the cards that will help you to remember what is most important for you to be addressing just now. You can use just one or several, letting them guide you to valuable questions. Take in the whole card, the word, picture and questions, letting them stir you up and help you be more fully present to yourself. We all need to learn how to ask ourselves good questions, too, in this therapeutic process, so notice the questions that attract you, and begin to write and collect your own questions. Asking questions will help you to move more deeply into yourself and into the subject you are addressing.

It is sometimes fun to share the card or cards you have picked with the whole class---then sharing a little of how it fit or didn't fit for you. When we use the cards in a face to face class we each take a few minutes to share our cards, and find that the sharing really does deepen the class, and helps everyone to open up just a little more. Sometimes another person's sharing can be very important.

A Glance Back---Since we are starting a new year it seems like a fitting time to do a brief review of the year just past. If you keep a journal or even a planner, you could go back to look at your life month by month. You could make notes to yourself about significant things as you review either your journal or just a regular calendar. I know I can be very surprised when I do this…realizing that I already had forgotten about achievements as well as disappointments. You could do your review from any perspective that fits for you just now---whether it be about health, work related concerns, celebrations, things you learned, what brought you energy or what depleted you, or just leaf through and see what pops up for you.

Take as much time as you need for this…and do it as quickly or as painstakingly as you desire. I'd recommend the middle ground—not too fast so as to miss a lot but also not too slow, or you may not keep your energy up to finish it. You might just write down each month and then your notes or a sentence about what stood out for you. Remember the idea is to "glance" back, not to get stuck in old stuff!

Having now completed that review, you have much more information at your fingertips that you can use---in this therapeutic way. Consider, for instance, how you feel having done that review? How do you feel about yourself, your life, and the year just past? Write a sentence or two about that. Are there specific happenings that you want to explore further—either in celebration or in release? Take one such event at a time, set your timer for ten minutes, and write about each topic that you want to pursue further. This is a good way to let go of "unfinished business" so you are free to be more present now.

Just for fun…imagine that you can change history---that you have a magic wand that will take any happening and make it different. What would you choose? Pick one and rewrite your life for that event. *Let your imagination help you make it just right!* Notice afterwards how you feel.

Make a list, next, of lessons learned over the last year. Just make a "bulleted" list of lessons. For example, I began exercising in earnest this year and so a first bullet might be:

- Learned the value of working in a gym with a trainer.

Another could be

- Realized that I love being a grandmother but still must be careful to take care of myself at the same time.

You might want to make a **List** of things you learned as well as another of things you hope to learn about over the next twelve months.

Next, still using the remembrances from your year's review, make a list of the people who have been most important to you, this year and further back, too, if you desire. You could have a "good" list and a "bad" one if you want, even though I believe even the difficult people are ultimately good for us—maybe even more so. After completing the list, pick one who you would like to think about more . . .

and write down their name. Then, follow this brief guided meditation and follow it with a description of your chosen person:

✦ Meditation ✦

Take a deep breath . . . and exhale. Do that again . . . and as you breathe in, imagine you are breathing in all the help and guidance and love that you could possibly need or want . . . and as you exhale just let go of all the unpleasant thoughts, feelings, energies that have gotten stuck inside…Continue this gentle breathing, enjoying the freeing feelings it brings to you.

Now, imagine that you are shifted into a new dimension . . . and as you sit there very quietly…you can see, or feel, or know that the person with whom you want to "visit" is nearby. Let images come to you of the environment where this person resides and of you both walking in the area . . . seeing each other from far away at first . . . still knowing that it is that person…and gaining a clearer perspective as he/she walks closer to you. This is a gentle meeting, and as you get closer and closer you see more and more of who this person is, how they look, what they are wearing and what kind of energy they bring with them.

Finally you are face to face . . . and you take your attention away from the person and put your awareness inside yourself as you notice how you feel in the presence of that person. Notice what feelings are evoked as you stand in this presence.

As you take your attention back to this person you once again get in touch with what is important to you about them . . . and you're able to find just the right words to help you express it all. If there are questions you want to ask this person, write those down, too, so that you can take some time, after writing a description of this experience, to hear—through your pen— what this person has to say in response to your question.

Breathe again, deeply, as you prepare to say goodbye for now to this person. Say goodbye . . . noticing your feelings . . . and, when you are ready, take another deep breath, pick up your pen and begin to write about what you imagined.

✦

Once you've finished your writing on this meditation, you've finished your exercises for the Session. You might want to continue . . . or to pick a **JournalCard** each day to give you more time to just *be* with yourself. There is no right or wrong way to do this journal writing, so just see what fits best for you and your life!

Session 2

I've found that folks generally do pretty well doing the first session, and then, sometimes, life gets in the way and it gets hard to keep up. I'm saying this now so you will know that there's no need to feel guilty if that happens. My suggestion: if you find yourself unable to take the time to do all the exercises, take five or ten minutes to respond to a **JournalCard**. That way you will keep your hand in the process, and will know that you can return to the exercises whenever you want.

As we start into Session 2, here is a quote from Eckhart Tolle's book, **Stillness Speaks.** He speaks eloquently on the subject of *now*, which is our focus for this Session.

> *"On the surface it seems that the present moment is only one of many, many moments. Each day of your life appears to consist of thousands of moments where different things happen. Yet if you look more deeply, is there not only one moment, ever? Is life ever not 'this moment'?*
> *"This one moment—Now—is the only thing you can never escape from, the one constant factor in your life. No matter what happens, no matter how much your life changes, one thing is certain: it's always Now.*
> *"Since there is no escape from the Now, why not welcome it, become friendly with it? When you make friends with the present moment, you feel at home no matter where you are. When you don't feel at home in the Now, no matter where you go, you will carry unease with you."*

We certainly can look back and reflect on where we have been, and at the same time, it is important that we don't get stuck there. Carolyn Myss, a medical intuitive, speaks of how we often spend far too much of our **now** energy focused on past events—often so much so that we have little energy left to be truly present. I know for myself that I spent a lot of time focused too much on the past, and so have resolved to be more present **now**.

I.   Begin your writing by taking time to again make the shift from outer focus to inner awareness. Write for about **five minutes** . . . and notice what flows from your pen. Is there something that needs to be released so you can feel more present? Experiment with being more and more honest as you write, making better and better friends with your journal and yourself.

II.   *JournalCards!* These cards can be used in a multitude of ways, one at a time, several, or in a series to explore a particular issue. As you look now at transitioning into a new year, let each card represent something different; the first card could suggest something about the past—something that is less important to you now than it used to be. The next card is about the present and something having to do with a current focus, and the last card represents something that is coming in the future. Keep a light hand and a light attitude as you play with the cards---and give yourself permission to experiment in this way-- or to use them as you have before, whatever fits best for you.

What do you need to let go of? Reflection is important, yet we don't want to get stuck looking back. Certain things must be released in order for us to be fully present. You may want to refer back to your review of the past year to see what you have and/or would like, to release.

III.   You could do this in the form of a **Cluster**. And when you've finished, take a moment or two to write about what you learned about what needs to be released. You may want to write key issues on a separate piece of paper so you can tear them up or burn them as a symbolic part of your releasing process.

Let's take some time now to take a look at what it means to you to feel fully alive. I see that as where your *passion* lies. When we feel passionate about something we are keenly aware of being alive and engaged.

IV.   Create an **Alphapoem** using the word *passion*.

P
A
S
S
I
O
N

V.   When you have completed that poem, look within it for another word or phrase that is "juicy" and use *that* word as the base for another **Alphapoem**.

VI.   Lastly, pick the place in your body where you identify the passion coming from. Use that place as the word or phrase that will be your third **Alphapoem** about passion in your life. Let your unconscious speak to you as you move through these three poems and just the right words pop up for you to use. Enjoy the process, and let go of trying to make it anything but what it is. If you want, write a sentence or two about what showed up for you—and how you felt about that technique as a therapeutic writing tool.

Right along with *passion*, I think, are *gratitudes*. It seems they go together; if we have passion we feel grateful, and if we are grateful we feel passion. It is always useful to stop and be aware of all you have to feel grateful about.

VII.   So start a fresh page in your journal and begin a sentence that says, "I am grateful for . . ." See how many ways you can finish that sentence. Try to extend it into a *long* **List**, numbering as you go, allowing yourself to repeat, and going at least to 50. It's even more revealing if you make your list to 100.

VIII.   For the next exercise I'd like to suggest that, with all that has now been stirred up within you, that you take some time to **write a prayer**---to whatever you believe in---offering your thanks as well as asking for assistance in whatever way you feel important. You may write it in the form of an **Unsent Letter**, just to give it some structure, and, if you want even imagine that a response comes to you from your Higher Power.

IX.   And lastly, again using the question posed by Ira Progoff in his journaling workshops, ask yourself, "What stirs?" and write your response.

Session 3

One of the topics that may prove very important for you is to **Ask Questions.** It seems that many folks lack good skills in question asking. I didn't learn how to ask important questions until I was in therapy, and then I realized that part of what I was learning from my therapist was *how to ask myself the important questions.* In fact, one of the underling purposes I had in mind when designing

JournalCards was to help people learn to ask their own questions---and for them to realize, too, that they have their own answers!

Recently, a student in my Phoenix College class told me that there is an infinite (almost) number of "quotes" available on the Internet. Quotes are often very useful as prompts for journaling, and so I was delighted to discover that I could look up "quotes + any topic" on Google and could feast on a seemingly inexhaustible supply. I spent some time doing just that, and here are a few of the quotes that showed up about questions:

Pablo Picasso:

"Computers are useless; they can only give you answers."

Paul Tillich:

"Being religious means asking passionately the question of the meaning of our existence and being willing to receive answers, even if the answers hurt."

Rainer Maria Rilke:

"Have patience with everything that remains unsolved in your heart. Try to love the questions themselves, like locked rooms and like books written in a foreign language. Do not now look for the answers. They cannot now be given to you because you could not live them. It is a question of experiencing everything. At present you need to live the question. Perhaps you will gradually, without even noticing it, find yourself experiencing the answer, some distant day."

Sam Keen:

"To be on a quest is nothing more or less than to become an asker of questions."

Sigmund Freud:

"Despite my thirty years of research into the feminine soul, I have not been able to answer the greatest question that has never been answered: What does a woman want?"

Soren Kierkegaard:

"Where am I? Who am I? How did I come to be here? What is this thing called the world? How did I come into the world? Why was I not consulted? And If I am compelled to take part in it, where is the director? I want to see him."

Thomas Jefferson:

"Question with boldness even the existence of a God; because if there be one, he must more approve of the homage of reason than that of blindfolded fear."

I. Pick one of these quotes as the prompt for your first **Five Minute Sprint**. Or write what you need to say in this moment, perhaps inspired by one of the quotes above. Use your own wisdom to discern what you need now.

II. Following the routine we have established throughout, pick one, two or three *JournalCards*. Notice the questions that you are attracted to, and consider how you might create your own *JournalCard* around your special topic (that can be an activity for another time). See what the questions you like bring up for you now, and take some time to respond in your journal.

III. Take a look at your history as a person who does or doesn't ask questions. I think this is useful for us to review, since I know for myself that as a child I was discouraged from asking questions by my family. I was too often the "good girl" and I feel as though I would have been better to have asked many more questions earlier on. I believe that questions give us confidence, suggest that we are responsible for ourselves, and also demonstrate that we are a constant "work in progress".

IV. To look into this, use the **Steppingstones** technique to allow yourself to get perspective on different topics. Progoff always suggested that **Steppingstones** be a list of 8 to 12 steps during one's life, and that it always begins with "I was born . . ." Simply let thoughts about yourself as a question asker emerge for you, one at a time. Mine might start like this:

- I was born into a family that needed to be in control . . .

- I was treated as dumb for asking questions . . .
- I lacked confidence as I went through school, trying to figure out how I "should" react and trying to be pleasing . . .
- I began to take more responsibility for my life and to ask important questions of myself, like why wasn't I happy . . . ?
- I entered counseling and had someone helping me ask important questions . . .
- I went to school to become a counselor and learned even more about how to ask questions . . .

- I realized that to be fully alive I had to continually work on my development and that meant asking questions . . .
- I began to teach others how to trust themselves to ask their own questions.

As I did that exercise, I realized that it might be difficult for you to do **Steppingstones** on this topic. If you can, good, but if it seems too fuzzy to discern your relationship to questions, try imagining yourself as an observer—like a friend or relative that has known you a long time—and let the "observer" tell you how you are at **Asking Questions**. This is a form of the technique called **Perspectives**, which allows you to imagine yourself as a different person or in a different place or time. Either **Steppingstones** or **Perspectives** can help you get closer to the notion of how much responsibility you take for asking yourself the right questions.

IV. Take about **five minutes** to write about your values about asking questions. Do you feel it's important to ask questions or not? Can you see the connection to asking good questions and moving forward effectively in your life? What, if any, resolutions do you want to make about asking yourself more questions? Are questions going to help you make a better Fresh Start? What questions are most important for you to be asking just now?

Moving forward—getting a Fresh Start! What part of your life stands out for you now as needing most of your energy and concentration of questions?

V. Write down three or four of your major goals . . . and then pick the one that is most important to you *now*. Write down the area of your life upon which you want to focus, and then, numbering as you go, *ask yourself as many questions as you can* to help get the information you need to move ahead. Don't worry about the answers just now . . . just deal with the questions. Make your **List** as long as you can, and even allow yourself to repeat questions---since that will help you to know which ones are really important to you.

VI. Ask for help. Write an **Unsent Letter** to a friend or mentor, living or dead, who can help you, both with good questions as well as good answers, to what confronts you now in your life. Ask this person for advice, inspiration, and whatever else you may need in order to take a step in your Fresh Start.

VII. Imagine this person now speaking through your pen . . . and giving you important words of wisdom. Then, continue this **Dialogue** by responding to what has been said. Write it as if a script, with you as one part and your wise helper as another part. Take it as far as you can and stretch, writing more and more questions, to help you gather more and more help.

Action steps! How can you make use of these insights to help you create an effective plan of action? After you have come up with some *Action Steps*, consider sharing your plans with at least one other person----it will help you to be more accountable to yourself.

Finally, as a little "bonus" for this session, capture an awareness of what questions get stirred up for you during the week, and write them down to use for extra journaling sessions.

Session 4

Well, here we are at the last segment of our Online Class. I hope you are feeling more comfortable with yourself as you have reviewed the year just past, taken a look at what you need to release, asked some questions about what needs to be addressed next, and now…perhaps you can begin to take some time to play with your imagination to see what else you want to create in your life!

Before you begin writing, go to your computer and visit this Internet link: http://www.beliefnet.com/story/3/story_385_1.html. It's a ten minute guided meditation, just another way to quiet yourself even more deeply before you do your therapeutic writing for this week.

I. Begin with writing for about **five minutes** about whatever is going on for you just now. Clear the air, so to speak, so you can reach further in to the safe and warm place you are creating as you write.

II. As you use your ***JournalCards*** this time, take *four* cards, paying attention to the order in which they were picked. This is another fun way to play with them and can often lead to interesting insights. Assign these meanings to the cards:

- #1 represents your mission in life.
- #2 is both your gift and your challenge in life.
- #3 is what is occurring for you in the present.
- #4 is something that lies ahead.

Have fun playing with these cards and seeing how they direct you toward what you know to be true about yourself and your life.

And now more lighthearted fun and play as you:

III. Create a picture (and some of you may want to actually draw it!) of how you would like your new, fresh life to look! See if you can combine being both somewhat realistic and also BOLD as you imagine your life and what is going on within it. We can't know when we've gotten what we want if we don't know what we want…so play with your picture!

IV. Now that you have that picture created for yourself, imagine that you can actually *step into it!* You are now *LIVING that reality!* Close your eyes for a few moments and imagine yourself there—seeing, feeling, smelling, touching and knowing---using all your senses, feeling exactly what it is like to be there. The more you can bring it into focus and feel your feelings of being there, the better you are able to PULL it into reality. Describe how it feels in complete detail. Write some more, *as you give this new life you have created a voice!* That may sound odd, but see if you can go with it . . . imagine that this new life can talk to you. Can it tell you what it needs in order to become real? What does it ask of you? What obstacles, if any, lie between where you are and creating this new space? In about five or six minutes of writing, take this conversation as far as you can, **Asking Questions** as appropriate.

V. Now, time to have some more fun with an **Alphapoem**, using the whole alphabet, about your *Fresh Start!* Describe this new life and what it brings you!

VI. Finish up by describing the actions you need to take to make your life dreams come true. Write for **five minutes**. When you're done, read what you have written, underlining key phrases that pull you forward. Pick one of those phrases and make it the title of another **Five Minute Sprint**. And again when done, read this passage through and pick out the most significant phrases. As you choose one it will become the title for your last **Five Minute Sprint**. You may discover that this work will lead you to even more wisdom about how to move ahead in your *Fresh Start.*

Project Eleven

"Who Has Their Finger On Your Remote?" – Exploring Personal Power

Whether you are participating as part of a group or as an individual, I know you will find these exercises to be stimulating for you. Remember, you can repeat these sessions and exercises as often as you like, and will find your responses will change each time you do—demonstrating our ongoing and ever changing process of growth.

We all have at least one remote sitting in our living rooms, whether it is for the TV, the DVD player or for your music system. It's become so handy to *push our little buttons* to control our environments more easily, and we are probably a little spoiled in terms of flicking our attention from one channel to the next. As we all become more automated some probably wonder some days if *we* have become little machines, (I know I do!) serving others in our lives. So the question, "Who holds *your* remote?" is a good one to consider—and within that is also the question about *whose remote **you** hold* as well. Hopefully, these exercises will help us all get clearer about how we can *more consciously control our own lives*—and how we can allow others control of theirs, too.

To give you a rough idea of the four sessions, you will first explore your own buttons—and who pushes them. Some quotes from ***Seven Habits of Highly Effective People*** by Stephen Covey will add some oomph to this discussion. Then we'll move into an inner discussion of what is really important to you, and what you are really good at. More help comes from Covey's book in that lesson, too. In our third session we'll look again at the obstacles we create to keep us from our power, and do some work on our inner critics and asking them to buzz off. An excerpt from **Power Vs. Force** by David Hawkins will offer even more food for thought. Finally, in the last session we'll use quotes and concepts from Stephen Levine's **A Year to Live** to help shift our awareness to more immediacy and personal empowerment. You'll be ready to more consciously take your remote back into your own control—and will give others their remotes back to control more of their own lives, too.

Session 1

I.   Let's begin! Find a comfortable place to sit (hopefully in a quiet space), and nestle in, remembering that you have no requirements to use correct grammar, spelling or punctuation. This is a time to just focus on what needs to be said . . . and what your pen directs you to write. Especially in this first **Five Minute Sprint**, you are simply "making the shift" from external awareness to inner awareness. It is most important just to begin, to respond to the simple question, "What's going on?" As you do that you will see yourself letting go of externally based issues and will begin to move your awareness toward where you are NOW. Set your timer for this five-minute exercise . . . as a way to warm up. Starting where you are always makes it easier to then move into deeper places within.

II.   Pick a **JournalCard**! As you use your own intuition to pick *just the right card* for where you are in this moment, you will find that as you connect you will move just a little more deeply into your own spirit . . . and your own magic. Don't try to answer all the questions, but simply allow yourself to relate to the word, the image or one of the questions on the card, noting how it is reminding you of something meaningful in your life. Again, my suggestion is to make it a 'timed writing' so you know that when you have written for five or ten or fifteen minutes (whatever you choose) you are done with this exercise. Of course it is up to you to decide how long you want to write, but timed writing is very helpful, especially to the new journal writer. As with *all* the exercises in these Projects, if there is some aspect of my suggestions that is uncomfortable to you . . . or just doesn't fit, then make changes in the directions. Do the exercise so that it works for you. That is the goal in all this work—that you explore your life in ways that are most rich and vital to you.

III. Soooo, who *does* push your buttons? Who has their finger on *your* remote? There are lots of answers that can come up for us . . . like our children, spouses, bosses, society's rules, religion . . . so let yourself just go with this idea. Make a **List**, as long as you can, allowing yourself to even repeat if you want. This will help you see which operatives are dominating your remote! Make your list at least to 25, maybe to 50, numbering as you go and writing quickly. You needn't yet distinguish between those you find positive and those more negative. Just see *who controls your time and energy*, being as *honest* as you can be. Let this be a brainstorming exercise—which means no censoring or judging who is on your list.

IV. Take a little time to look over your results. Write about what comes to you as you consider who controls you and your time. This is not a time for heavy evaluation, just a chance to reflect, again now more deeply, into where your power goes—and whether that works well for you. What are the positives and the negatives for you about others managing your remote?

I would add that, as Carolyn Myss suggests, it can be useful to imagine that we each have 100 units of energy available to us daily. If we use our power only in the service of others, without 'refueling' ourselves, what do you imagine will happen? As you see how you "spend" your energy, consider how *your* power is funded.

V. What kind of "remote" or person are you? Are you one who responds to the touch of everyone else in your life? Do you feel little control over yourself and your time or lots of control? Think about a situation when you felt either that you allowed someone else to control you or a time when you heard what another was asking but chose to remain true to your own wants/needs? Try this short meditation of those scenarios now to help you focus and describe what happens for you.

✦ Meditation ✦

Take a deep breath . . .
*Let your eyes soften . . . relax your body completely, and give yourself a moment to **see** the picture of that experience in your minds eye. **Feel** how you felt, **notice all your senses** and*

> *what they are telling you . . .*
> *As you again take a deep breath, allowing the whole situation*
> *to appear before you in your mind, let the words and images*
> *flow effortlessly from your inner knowing . . .*
> *and then down your arm and through your pen . . .*
> *Describe in detail this experience and how you felt about it. Did*
> *you give away your power . . .*
> *your 'remote,' or did you hold on?*
>
> ✦

As always, don't worry about the grammar or spelling, but allow yourself to simply express the situation as you now remember it.

At this point, I think it would be helpful to share a little information with you from Stephen Covey's book, **Seven Habits . . ."** He doesn't write about being a "remote" but does talk about being proactive or reactive. I always find it useful to review this material even though many of us are already familiar with it.

> *"While the word proactivity is now fairly common in management literature, it is a word you won't find in most dictionaries. It means more than merely taking initiative. It means that as human beings, we are responsible for our own lives. Our behavior is a function of our decisions, not our conditions. We can subordinate feelings to values. We have the initiative and the responsibility to make things happen.*
> *"Look at the word responsibility—"response-ability"—the ability to choose your response. Highly proactive people recognize that responsibility. They do not blame circumstances, conditions, or conditioning for their behavior. Their behavior is a product of their own conscious choice, based on values, rather than a product of their conditions, based on feelings.*
> *"Because we are, by nature, proactive, if our lives are a function of conditioning and conditions, it is because we have, by conscious decision or by default, chosen to empower those things to control us.*
> *"In making such a choice we become reactive. Their physical environment often affects reactive people. If the weather is good, they feel good. If it isn't, it affects their attitude and their performance. Proactive people can carry their own weather with them. Whether it rains or shines makes no difference to them. They are value driven; and if their*

value is to produce good quality work, it isn't a function of whether the weather is conducive to it or not.

"Reactive people are also affected by their social environment, by the 'social weather.' When people treat them well, they feel well, when people don't, they become defensive or protective. Reactive people build their emotional lives around the behavior of others, empowering the weaknesses of other people to control them.

"The ability to subordinate an impulse to a value is the essence of the proactive person. Reactive people are driven by feelings, by circumstances, by condition, by their environment. Proactive people are driven by values—carefully thought about, selected and internalized values.

"Proactive people are still influenced by external stimuli, whether physical, social, or psychological. But their response to the stimuli, conscious or unconscious, is a value-based choice or response.

"As Eleanor Roosevelt observed, 'No one can hurt you without your consent.' In the words of Ghandi, 'They cannot take away our self respect if we do not give it to them.' It is our willing permission, our consent to what happens to us, that hurts us far more than what happens to us in the first place.

"And I admit this is very hard to accept emotionally, especially if we have had years and years of explaining our misery in the name of circumstance or someone else's behavior. But until a person can say deeply and honestly, 'I am what I am today because of the choices I made yesterday,' that person cannot say, 'I choose otherwise.'" (pp. 70–72)

VI.   Take some time now, to write an **Unsent Letter** to *yourself*, describing how you have been either reactive or proactive or both. Talk to yourself as though talking to your best friend, offering help, support, comfort and understanding for what has been. At the same time, consider what kind of support you may offer to this 'friend' as you move ahead.

VII. Create some kind of *Action Step* that will help 'your friend' to be more responsible and more proactive in her/his life. Use this as a time to say whatever needs to be said in a gentle and supportive fashion.

VIII. Pick out one, two or three people from your first list—those who control your 'remote.' One at a time, write each of them an **Unsent Letter** that describes how you have let them have too much control over you (if they have) and how that is now going to change. Make this a win-win exercise, understanding that *each* of us must be responsible for ourselves first. Then and only then can we be useful to others. If we support one another in that process we can *all* be better off.

IX.   What stirs? See where you stand, how you feel. Take some time to simply note and reflect on how you now feel. You've covered a lot of territory in this session, so give yourself a pat on the back for staying with it.

Session 2

Have you been paying more attention to who "has their finger on your remote" since doing the prior session? I hope so. It's important to be able to take the information that you have processed for yourself in your journaling back into your life. This journaling is so much more than just writing. We are, in a way, identifying and describing our values, what is important to us, and what we need to do in order to be even more successful. One step at a time we become more conscious and aware of how we are in our world . . . vs. how we really *want* to be. You are all—all those of you who are participating in these exercises—courageous and responsible people. Keep up the good work.

I.   As you begin your first exercise in this week's session, your **Five-Minute Sprint**, see what slides out from your pen as you write. It may be related to the material from the previous lesson, or it may be about something that has grabbed your attention *today!* Whatever it is, just begin, and feel the "shift" that helps you let go of the externals and move into your inner awareness's. Don't judge what comes out but just allow yourself to be present and aware of what is going on. Enjoy.

II.   Continue to honor your needs and concerns of the moment as you draw a *JournalCard* or two to help you with focus. Let the cards help stir you up, so that you can continue to move beyond the surface of your life and into the concerns that need your time and attention. As you add one or two cards to the original one you pick you'll see more meaning and more depth appear for you. Go with them and notice how, if at all, you move beyond your initial thoughts. See how writing is 'different' than just thinking, and offers the opportunity to 'see' even more than we would have thought possible. (Be sure to breathe as you do these exercises as it helps you to open, release, relax and refresh.)

Just *where and how* do you experience yourself as *powerful* in your life today? Just the fact that you keep a journal says that you know a lot about being responsible for your own life. Many of us (myself especially) who are reflective are also very hard on ourselves. The power we have we may deny—and fail to honor the ways in which we do act in powerful and effective ways.

III.   Sometimes it is the smaller, more 'ordinary' ways that we exercise our power. Maintaining a household, responding to phone calls and emails, keeping ourselves healthy by exercising, holding down a job . . . all are examples of ways that we express our personal power. Make a short list to begin with. Then pick one to explore more fully.

Give yourself permission to describe one way that you are powerful in your life. As you did in last week's exercises, give yourself time to be quiet and breathe into your feelings about how you have acted with power. My hope is that as we learn to better support ourselves we will more easily operate in a proactive way from our power. Use as many descriptive words as you can in this exercise.

Here again are some excerpts from **Seven Habits of Highly Effective People** to help you think about what IS important to you and how you may begin thinking about creating your own Mission Statement.

> *"A personal mission statement based on correct principles . . . becomes a personal constitution, the basis for making major, life-directing decisions, the basis for making daily decisions in the midst of the circumstances and emotions that affect our lives. It empowers individuals with the same timeless strength in the midst of change.*
>
> *"People can't live with change if there's not a changeless core inside them. The key to the ability to change is a changeless sense of who you are, what you are about and what you value.*
>
> *"With a mission statement, we can flow with changes. We don't need prejudgments or prejudices. We don't need to figure out everything else in life, to stereotype and categorize everything and everybody in order to accommodate reality.*
>
> *"Once you have that sense of mission, you have the essence of your own pro-activity. You have the vision and the values that direct your life. You have the basic direction from which you set your long and short-*

> *term goals. You have the power of a written constitution based on correct principles, against which every decision concerning the most effective use of your time, your talents, and your energies can be effectively measured." (p. 108–109)*

He goes on later describing more about personal Mission Statements:

> *"As proactive people, we can begin to give expression to what we want to be and to do in our lives. We can write a personal mission statement, a personal constitution.*
>
> *"A mission statement is not something you write overnight. It takes deep introspection, careful analysis, thoughtful expression, and often many rewrites to produce it in final form.*
>
> *"I find the process is as important as the product. Writing or reviewing a mission statement changes you because it forces you to think through your priorities deeply, carefully, and to align your behavior with your beliefs. As you do, other people begin to sense that you're not being driven by everything that happens to you. You have a sense of mission about what you're trying to do and you are excited about it." (p. 129)*

IV. Consider what would be part of your Personal Mission Statement, just a rough draft to help you begin to identify your core beliefs and concerns. To help you in this exploratory process I suggest that you go through ALL of your *JournalCards*. Pick out the ones that really speak to you now about your core beliefs. List them in your journal. Create a sentence or two using them all. Read it over and see how you want to change it to better reflect what is most important to you—your own "personal constitution."

Here is an example of a Mission Statement: ***"My mission is to live with integrity and to make a difference in the lives of others."*** (p. 136)

As you can see, a mission statement ultimately can be very simple, but the process of getting it there may take awhile.

While creating this project I have thought again about my own Mission Statement. My rough draft goes like this: ***"On a daily basis, my mission is to creatively expand, using my power, with balance, to prayerfully add to the quality of life for myself and those I am in touch with. I believe in the magic within each of us that helps us all to achieve far beyond our imagining—and appreciate the community within which that magic expands."*** So you see how a rough draft can be really rough . . . and may take a long time to sort through to distill down to a single sentence.

V. All of this activity may seem difficult to you. This kind of work, of digging deeply within, takes a lot of energy. Sometimes it is helpful to have assistance, so for now, make a list of those people, living and dead, who have loved, supported, nurtured and inspired you. Imagine all of them on your *team* helping you become clear and focused about who you are, what's important to you and where you are going. These are probably people who do not try to take your power but rather try to help you realize your own. After you have written each name, write one adjective that best describes them next to their name.

VI. Now, using the power of your *team*, pick one as a spokesperson, who can speak to you now and offer you love, guidance and support. You can begin this exercise either by imagining what this person has to say to you directly, or you may begin as a **Dialogue** by asking a question. This team member may speak as an individual or for the whole group. Let this conversation go just as long as you desire. Take a nice deep breath as you switch back and forth from this person to your self and back again. Your Dialogue can continue as long as you desire, writing it as though it were a script.

While you are now hopefully feeling the support that surrounds you both in real time and through the contacts you have made over the years, how can you now begin . . . or take another step forward in fulfilling your Mission Statement? Covey talks about this too—"*How we are going to fulfill our mission?*" In other words, once you have decided what guides you in your life, how will you take action to accomplish that goal or mission?

So consider that for yourselves now. What must you do in your life to assure yourself that you can move—or continue to move—in the direction of satisfying your goals? Perhaps you gained some insight in your previous exercise with your supportive team member.

VII. Make a **List** or create a **Cluster** to help you brainstorm the changes or new focus you need to take. Pick one, then, that is very doable, and turn it into an *Action Step*. You may choose to take one more step, which is telling your Journal Group (if you have one) of your plan, so that you feel some sense of accountability for following through on your plan.

VIII. Now, imagine that you have been successful in fulfilling your Mission Statement. Pretend, for the sake of this exercise, that it is exactly *one year* from now. You are about to make a **Perspectives** entry in your journal, describing all that has gone on in the last year particularly in respect to your Mission Statement, and how that has changed your focus and helped you to be much more clear about yourself, your life and your activities. Write today's date for *next year* and begin a journal entry, reporting on all the changes (and success) you have had in the last year.

(By the way, you may find that as you keep your journals and then take a little time periodically to review them, that you will see how many of your goals you actually do achieve. I have been personally surprised to see how much of what I say I want I actually achieve . . . and in shorter and shorter amounts of time now between dream and actuality. Check it out for yourself!)

Session 3

My hope is that you are continuing to notice more about "who is holding your remote" even when you are not journaling. Becoming more conscious is an ongoing process and our journals make wonderful companions in which to ask the questions, make observations, pledge changes, see movement, and celebrate successes. Please take time to **Freewrite**—just to write as though talking to yourself, anytime you have something noteworthy to record. It is for you to do as you, in a sense, learn to become your own coach or mentor.

So *what do you notice* about who you give your power to? Or do you maintain a healthy balance most of the time? What does it even mean to be powerful? Often in classes I find people react negatively to the word power, seeing it as something that has been used against others. I found a book from which I will share more information, to offer the way I find most useful in looking at power and what it means. The book is called **_Power Vs. Force_** and was written by David Hawkins. Here is a brief excerpt:

> *"On examination, we'll see that power arises from meaning. It has to do with motive, and it has to do with principle. Power is always associated with that which supports the significance of life itself. It appeals to that part of human nature that we call noble—in contrast to force, which appeals to that which we call crass. Power appeals to what uplifts, dignifies, and ennobles. Force must always be justified, whereas power requires no justification. Force is associated with the partial, power with the whole.*

"If we analyze the nature of force, it becomes readily apparent why it must always succumb to power; this is in accordance with one of the basic laws of physics. Because force automatically creates counter-force, its effect is limited by definition. We could say that force is a movement—it goes from here to there (or tries to) against opposition. Power, on the other hand, is still. It's like a standing field that doesn't move. Gravity itself, for instance, doesn't move against anything. Its power moves all objects within its field, but the gravity field itself does not move.

"Force always moves against something, whereas power doesn't move against anything at all. Force is incomplete and therefore has to be fed energy constantly. Power is total and complete in itself and requires nothing from outside. It makes no demands; it has no needs. Because force has an insatiable appetite, it constantly consumes. Power, in contrast, energizes, gives forth, supplies, and supports. Power gives life and energy—force takes these away. We notice that power is associated with compassion and makes us feel positively about ourselves. Force is associated with judgment and makes us feel poorly about ourselves." (pp. 132–133)

What this suggests to me is that, just as Covey has described, if we are driven by our principles and are proactive, we will operate from our own power, and have no need of force. We will harmonize with those around us, cooperating in a way that creates a win-win scenario for all. Our power will free us to be able to live more peacefully, more creatively and with more healing *power*. So, let's move on to our exercises:

I. Begin again with a **Five-Minute Sprint**. Note what is going on for you right now. Are you caught up in some life drama . . . or have you had time to already begin your "shift" into more inner awareness? What, if any, thoughts do you have about your power and how you impact the world you live in? Stay with where you are now, without judging, just knowing that in order to get where you want to go— into greater wisdom—you must first be where you are. It's like following any map—you can't know what route to take to your destination unless you know where you are starting from!

II. *JournalCards*—Pick one *JournalCard*, and take it in . . . absorbing the word, picture and questions into your life situation now. Feel how, if at all, it fits for you. If you like, take another card, letting it augment your first one, and helping you expand your understanding of where you are and what you need.

These cards help us, I believe, in a non-judging way, to get a grip on aspects of our lives that may be just below our conscious awareness. As we *allow* the cards to assist us we can focus more clearly, more honestly . . . and ultimately more powerfully, on our central issues. I hope you will continue to use them even after our classes are through.

Part of what brings us to these therapeutic writing projects is the desire to become more aware, healthier, and to use our inner gifts more fully. So it makes sense that we become aware of who is "pushing our buttons," and whether we want to accept things as they are or if we want to make changes. As we begin to change we will *always* run into resistance from people and systems outside of us who want things to be the same as always.

III. Take some time now, either in a **List** or by creating a **Cluster**, to examine the obstacles you are encountering or have encountered—or anticipate encountering—as you assume more of your personal power.

Our obstacles to greater personal power may come from people and circumstances *outside of ourselves,* to whom we are still giving our power. Or, the obstacles may come *from the inside.* Ultimately, they are all *inner values* that we carry, even if we see them as influences from outside ourselves.

Many of us have a very active Inner Critic or Inner Judge, who is constantly telling us how we *should* be doing. This Critic becomes a common voice, and often we begin to think that the voice within is right. We can easily move into self-doubt and self-criticism. Does this sound like you? It's important to understand that *the critic is only a part of you* and does not dominate, even though it feels as though it does.

IV. Take some time now, in a non-judgmental way, to describe ways that you see your inner critic "holding your remote." Sometimes our critic, like our parents when we were small, just wants to try to protect us. However, like over protective parents, we can become stifled and unable to use our most profound gifts when saddled with unnecessary "shoulds" from our inner critics.

For this exercise, begin a **Dialogue** with your inner critic. You may begin by asking it why it is there. When you have imagined the response of this critic, then ask again, if it will step aside, so you can make some necessary changes. See how the critic responds. Can you agree to work together? Try referring back to your Mission

Statement, letting your critic know what is most important to you in your life. Experiment with this technique even if it feels a little awkward at first. Remember your journal is just for you and no one else will know of your experiment with talking to your inner critic.

V.   In your next journal exercise, allow yourself to create a prayer or request to whatever Higher Power you believe in. Ask for assistance in allowing your power to be expressed for your highest good. Take whatever awarenesses you've gained so far and ask that they be expanded so you can see more of your gifts and less of your limitations.

As you write your prayer, you may even decide you want to create a **Dialogue** with your Higher Power, just as you did with your critic. Equal time seems like the right thing to do!

In a recent newsletter, Susan Lark, MD, talks about how we so often are self-critical. She even points out how the immune system can be compromised by repeated attacks against ourselves. She supports the idea that we must learn to reprogram ourselves, dumping the emotional issues that hold us back, including the inner critic, and instead fill ourselves with self-love. She quotes the **Institute of HeartMath** in Boulder Creek, CA, with this exercise:

"Place your hand on your heart, let your eyes soften their focus, and think of someone or something you love very much.
Just focus on that person or thing until the corners of your mouth begin to curl upward in a smile.
Notice that your heart rate has slowed, your muscles are no longer tense, and you have relaxed.
Telling yourself that you are to be counted as a loved one, place yourself in the same scene in which you'd imagined the special person in step 2. Bask in the warm, relaxed glow of your heart's love, and say, "I am worthy." Say it not with anger or resentment but with compassion. When you feel emotion welling up in your eyes, you'll know that the message got in. "

For more information log onto www.heartmath.com.

VI.   What is it that you need to release now? Are there old programs, old beliefs that you now can see are no longer serving you? Try saying goodbye to the harshness of your critic, your belief in being perfect, your too high expectations of yourself. Try just writing this sentence:

"I am releasing . . ." and finish it in as many ways as you can. Write quickly, allow yourself to repeat, and notice how you feel as you really release old baggage that no longer fits.

VII. Along the same lines. Whenever we empty something from ourselves we need to have something else to add in. So allow yourself to freely and spontaneously finish the sentence, "I take my power back to . . ." and see how many ways you can respond to that sentence. Again, notice how you feel as you take your power back within you.

VIII. What stirs? As you read over your responses to the latest exercises, notice what comes up for you and how you feel. What stirs?

Session 4

Can you accept more of your power now? Can you feel it and not give it away so easily? Do you have a sense of feeling more alive? I hope so.

To begin our last session in this project, I want give you a little taste of a book by one of my heroes, Stephen Levine. The book is called **One Year to Live** and is based on his work with the dying for over twenty years. It is not a sad book, however, but rather one for those of us who are not yet facing death to more ardently grab the life we do have.

What Stephen found in his work with the dying was that many, when given a diagnosis that promised a shortened life span felt a freedom to do just what they really wanted to do. I have had the honor of working with many people who have been diagnosed with cancer and have made similar choices. Here's a taste of his perspective.

> "Most of us live half-unborn. Perhaps that is why so many have said that when they received their 'one year, last year' prognosis, they felt something tighten and then release in their gut. Somehow, beyond anything they imagined might occur in such circumstances, after the fear, an unexpected sense of spaciousness arose. One person said, 'As what the doctor said really sank in I could feel something very heavy begin to live. I felt as though I was free to live my life at last. Bizarrely, life never felt so safe. Maybe I'm crazy, but I felt more freedom and love than I had in some time. In fact, I felt not as though my life was being taken away but as though it had been given back to me. I was going to die and my life was completely my own.'

"I wondered what this new aliveness was that we see so often in those with only a few months to live. What boundaries have been lifted so noticeably that previous hindrances to joy and mercy toward self and others melt into an increasingly expanding awareness and appreciation of the present?

"Approaching a new year . . . it occurred to me that a New Year's Resolution Without Parallel would be to make a commitment to live my next year as if it were my last."

I.   Take some time to write about what you are thinking and feeling just now, without rehearsing, just letting your thoughts and feelings flow. See where this exercise takes you as you release yourself into the *now*. Feel the shift occur as you begin to move more deeply within yourself and your own inner magic.

II.   *JournalCards*–Go ahead a see what your *JournalCards* want to show you about yourself and your life just now. How do the questions help you get more honest with yourself and move a little more deeply within? Enjoy the process of seeing *more* of who you truly are.

III.   "Imagineering" is a term I use for a series of three exercises. Begin with describing how you feel just now about yourself, about who is holding your remote, and about your relationship to your own power. Let the time you have spent on these exercise just bring the bubbles of awareness and knowing to the surface.

- As the second part of this "**Imagineering,**" give yourself permission to describe the way you would like to be operating in your life, with a good balance of power, as you give and take in just the proportions you desire. If you want, you can draw a picture of this idealized life in your journal too, remembering that the same 'rules' apply to drawing as to writing—no need to do it in any special way.

- Now, as the third part of this imagining, you can imagine *stepping into the picture you have created*. As you step in you begin to feel the energy shift as you feel the changes going on in and around you. As you imagine waking up to start a new day in this new life, describe what happens as you take your new sense of self through your day. How does your experience of yourself, and of your own personal power change? Describe in great detail.

IV.   Going back to Stephen Levine's book premise, can you imagine how you might change your behaviors if you had a limited time to live (as we all do!)? Take the power you imagined in your last exercise. Imagine that you have one year to live. What will you keep in your life and what will you eliminate? What happens to you as you imagine that process?

V.   What stirs? Where are you now…and what is emerging as a primary *Action Step* for you as you move toward holding your own remote more of the time. Enjoy your new-found power.

Project Twelve

Visualize Your Success . . .
And Make It So!

In this project, the exercises we've built will help you to move into a more intimate awareness of yourself—what values you have, what you enjoy, what you dislike—and where you are going. All of that begins to shine through as you reflect on your life from different vantage points that these therapeutic writing sessions provide.

In this series, you'll begin as usual with "where are you now?" and move into deeper personal wonderings as you pick **JournalCards** to see how they help you to see your lives more clearly. From there you will explore the whole notion of "***success***" and what it means to you—and how you can take more steps to get where you want to be.

◆ *This exploration will be interesting—and can be even more so with the comments and feedback from your fellow group members, if you are doing it with a group. Of course it's important to remember that in journaling each person is their own best expert, and each is respected for their own perspective and chosen pathway. As group members share, however, new ideas may show themselves to you and new openings may occur. Remember to trust your instincts and change any exercise to best fit your own needs and direction, since all these exercises are just suggestions and not to be taken as carved in stone.*

Session 1

I.   Begin where you are. Find a comfortable spot and write, for only about **five minutes**, about what you are going through right now. What do you feel, what do you want, what are you not facing, what needs to be released? Choose any of those questions, or make up your own, to help you make room to be more fully present to yourself right now. Let this help you to 'shift' from external focus to inner awareness (where your true strength and wisdom lie).

II.   Pull a *JournalCard* now, asking to be reminded of what is important to hold in your awareness. It's funny how your *JournalCard* picks are often so fitting. However, if you can't make a good connection with your card, pick another—this is not a religious experience! Let those questions, or the picture, guide you into more and deepened reflection about your life now. You may even find it relates somehow to success—or to something that partially keeps you from getting where you want to be. Just explore and enjoy. Again, I recommend you set your timer and write for only five or ten minutes. Do *not* try to answer all the questions on the card but just let the card *stir you up* so you can reach further into your mind and heart.

◈ *Your **JournalCards** are a good thing to share with other group members—just talking about the card you pulled and then can decide how much or how little you may want to tell others about how it assisted you in moving to deeper places.*

III.   Begin to create a description of how your life will look when you are successful. You may, in fact, already be there. What does success include for you and how do you see yourself moving forward? If there is a word you like better than success, go ahead and use it. You are here to explore how to move forward in your life, and how to create the vision for the life you want to live, whatever you call it.

- One suggestion I have for this exercise is to go through your *JournalCards* one at a time, to pick out the ones you think are most important to your own version of successful living. They may help you to 'see' more clearly what you want.

- This is just the beginning for this question, so don't worry that you have to think of everything *now*. Just start with where you are. As you proceed through these exercises you will gain more and more clarity.

- You may now even find it helpful and easier to describe those things that you know you *don't* want in your life. You can do this exercise in a **Cluster** format—start with a circle in the center of the page and brainstorm from there, about **"My Life Vision"** or **"What I *Don't* Want in My Life."**

The *Merriam Webster Dictionary* defines success as "satisfactory completion of something" or "the gaining of wealth and fame." I find that quite enlightening, since our culture seems to have made success all about wealth and fame. The first definition is about completion in a satisfying way—and there seems to me to be a big difference between those definitions.

IV.   So now it's time to think about your own definition of success. What are your experiences with success? Or who are your models for success? This will force you to begin to define what that means to you, so as you begin to think of people and experiences that have been successful, notice what message they send to you. Make a short **List** of everyone you can think of that you see as successful. Include in that list your own experiences of success. Add in especially those people you most admire for their success and perhaps the way that they got there.

V.   Once you have completed your **List**, write out your own "working definition" for success. Then, pick the person or experience that is most *vibrant and alive* for you from your **List**. Describe in detail everything you can think of that makes *this* example so important and relevant to you. What makes *this* story a success story? Perhaps a particular kind of success is more important to you now than success that you achieved in the past. Dig in and explore.

VI.   Now, from the previous exercise, imagine that you are *in the presence of the success that you described.* If it is a person, you are in a meeting with them. If it is an old success story, you are back in that time, and the completion has a voice of its own.

Now you will begin a **Dialogue** with that person or that time, and will ask whatever question seems most relevant to you. Notice, as you imagine talking to this person, how you feel in their presence? Are they comforting, warm, inviting or cold and distant?

In writing your **Dialogue** it's easiest to begin with a question. Ask them if *they* feel successful, or how they define success. Then you may want to ask for advice for yourself. Just relax and be open to both sides of this conversation. Open to the idea that you really know more that you think you know.

It's important in choosing the person you will work with, that it is someone that you can *feel* to be on your side. You can bring this person with you throughout our month long exercises. At any time you may want to return to **Dialogue** with him/her as new questions pop up and new advice is needed.

VII.   Read through all that you have written on this topic to date. As you sift through the comments you made, what stands out to you? What have you realized? Do you feel more or less successful after getting clearer about your definition? Make note of any questions that come up for you, writing them in the back of your journal so you will have them ready for you when you have some free time to journal more, taking advantage of the wisdom you carry within.

Session 2

I.   As usual, begin with where you are and write for just about **five minutes**. As you do that you begin to make that 'shift' from external awareness to inner awareness, and from here you will begin your deepening process. As you deepen you move further and further into your own 'magic.'

II.   *JournalCards*. Pick one, two or three *JournalCards* to give you some focus, direction and guidance about what is most important in your life right now. What does this have to do with success, if anything? Write again for just a few minutes, five or ten, and do not try to answer all the questions, but pick the one that is most relevant to you and your life today. You will experience a greater sense of focus and that you have moved into a deeper part of yourself.

III.   Next, do a quick review. Think about your week, read over what you wrote in the last session and consider how you have thought about yourself and this concept of success over time. Or consider whether you have thought about it at all! Let that tell you something about the importance of achievement and success in your life up to now. Pay attention to any subtle changes that may have occurred in your thinking, or how you act in regard to others you view as successful.

IV.   Describe again, more fully now, and with more emotion included in it, your *vision* of how you want your life to be next. In what way do you want to achieve something, and how would the completion of that goal or goals bring you a feeling of success? Be as complete in this *vision* as you can be this time, going into more detail that you did in the last session. You may want to close your eyes for a while as you imagine it all happening. As you do that *feel* the emotion of it, *know* that it is happening as you sit there and then begin to *write* with that feeling and emotion also flowing from your pen. This is a time to *open up* any clogs and though you may see the obstacles you also *know* that you will find a way around them. . . . *Feel* the completion as much as you can, drawing that energy to you. . . . and enjoy the process as you put yourself *there*, having *made* it happen. You have co-created your future and know that you will continue to move ahead. Write on!

V.   I would suggest, additionally, that you type up and print out this *vision* so you can read it over often, remember each time the emotion of having completed that task successfully and moved into the next phase of your life.

VI. Write, either in prose form or in a **Cluster**, what you see as the *obstacles* to your completion of your goals and your ultimate success. Spell them out, and rate them 1–10 in terms of their complexity or difficulty in overcoming them. Be honest with yourself. Be as honest as you can be. Think about how much control you have over your obstacles.

VII. Write a brief prayer or **Unsent Letter**, to whatever power you believe in, inviting help for getting around, though, or redefining these obstacles. To the degree that you can, open your heart as you write, trusting that there are answers available that you simply are not yet aware of.

VIII. Now, return to your Session 1 exercises and re-read your **Dialogue** with your Mentor for success. Then, read over what you wrote this week about your *vision* for success. Combine the feelings from these pieces, along with your request for assistance in your prayer or **Unsent Letter**. With *all* these energies combining to help you, close your eyes briefly and ask for the wisdom to see beyond your obstacles. Then, write down each obstacle, and after it, allow those voices of wisdom to come forward, helping you to see more clearly that which you have been unable to see or to accept. Do this with each obstacle you can see in your way to complete success and fulfillment. Open, as you write, breathing deeply and *trusting* that just what you need will come to you.

Some answers or new perspective may come to you in your dreams or as you walk through your daily life. Simply be sure to make notes about these insights that come to you, and add them later to your journal work.

Session 3

I.   Hopefully, by now you realize the importance of starting your journal session in the present, just where you are. So, begin now and write about what has your attention and what you need to get out of the way in order to be fully present. Write for only **five minutes** and feel the shift occurring.

II. Want to use your *JournalCards* in a little different way? This time you can pull one or two as you have before, or you can try this additional exercise. Write down a question that you have about yourself or your life today. It can be about this issue of success or about anything else that is of concern to you. Write down your question. Then, take a deep breath and pick three cards, noting the order in which they were picked.

- Let the first card represent the situation as it is in your life now.
- Let the second card represent an action that would be good to take in relation to that situation
- The third card represents the new situation arising after the *Action Step* is taken.

See how this fits for your problem or your question and let it guide you to the wisdom that is right there inside you.

III. This exercise will help you to "lock in" even more the components to success and fulfillment for you. Make a **List**, numbering as you go, to 100—of all those things that you include as part of success. You will include physical things as well as feelings and beliefs. When you do this kind of exercise, in order to dip into your subconscious, it's important that you do it all in one sitting. It is a kind of brainstorming and will allow you to more fully *feel* what your success is like. Write quickly for this list, you *may* repeat yourself, and be sure to number as you go. Write quickly and do not censor your ideas. When you are through with your list you may want to note those things that you repeated—in as much as the repetition indicates more intense feelings about these things for you.

IV. This exercise will utilize the information from the previous exercise and will help you to deepen your awareness and understanding of how you feel and what you desire in your search for success.

- From the last exercise, choose one to three primary characteristics or feelings you have selected as most meaningful to you about your *vision* of success. My recommendation is to start with a feeling about how you will feel with this success that you desire. Then, make that the *title* for the first **Five Minute Sprint** you will write in this "**Series of Three**" exercise. Write for just five minutes on this topic, exploring it and your feelings and what success means to you, more fully.

- When you are through, underline those key words or phrases that are most "juicy" or meaningful to you. Let one of those then be the title for your next **Five Minute Sprint**.

- Again, underline key words or phrases, letting the most powerful one be the title for the third and last **Five Minute Sprint**.

V. Read over what you have written and write about any new perspectives or insights you gained through this "**Series of Three**." You may want to comment on the process and how it worked for you—especially if it has helped you see that you CAN trust more in answers that are available to you. Breathe into your work and pat yourself on the back for this deepening process you have gone through.

Session 4

I. Begin with where you are, writing for just **five minutes** and making that "shift" from external awareness to internal knowing. Acknowledge your successes, small or large as you write.

II. With your *JournalCards*, pick one, two or three cards to see what appears and how they help remind you about something important in your life. Write for 5 or 10 minutes about what they suggest to you.

- When you have completed that exercise, go back through your *JournalCards*, this time picking one to three cards that you see as integral to your success. Just put them out in front of you as you proceed through these exercises.

III.   Now you are going to use the technique called **Perspectives,** and in doing so are going to jump ahead, using your imagination. Now you are going to imagine yourself as ***having already achieved the success you desire.*** Give yourself some time to move into this space, reading over your *vision* again and feeling your body shift into the knowing of already being just where you want to be. The feelings that come make you different . . . and you hold yourself differently, more confidently . . . and you have more lightness in your being. Breathe deeply, close your eyes if you want, and really ***feel*** yourself there. You have successfully moved beyond whatever obstacles were there before.

   From this place, describe a day in your life, beginning with getting up in the morning, describing your home, your breakfast, how you leave for work, where you work and how you feel there. You talk about your significant relationships, your talents and gifts, and what ever else is part of your day as you live in this new dimension of complete success, peace and harmony. Enjoy the process.

IV.   Carry this fun feeling with you, and write the alphabet vertically down the left hand side of a new page—the whole alphabet! Then, create an **Alphapoem** about your new life. Remember to have fun with this, to not think too hard, and to not try to be perfect! That's not necessary in your new life of success!

◆ *Enjoy—and share the **Alphapoem** with those in your group if you desire!*

V.   From this heightened place of success and greater awareness, look back and see what awareness you have about what kept you stuck before. What kept you from this place? What advice would you offer your stuck self (the part of you that isn't there yet)? As you sit in this higher level of consciousness, what do you know that you didn't know when you were stuck in your smaller self?

   Additionally, what advice would you give to others who are seeking success? See if you can create a list of steps that you and others can take to insure greater peace and greater accomplishments in the future.

VI.   Finally, offer a prayer of gratitude for all that you have achieved, learned and accepted. Let your prayer include *everyone* you can think of who has been part of your growth, those you have liked as well as those you have not liked so well. Recognize as you write, the interconnectedness of us all. Ask for and offer forgiveness to all those you previously saw as part of the problem. Let your prayer sing to *all that is* of your joy and happiness!

VII.   Consider perhaps, what *Action Step* you can take to help others that are less fortunate than yourself. Once secure in prosperity what is your obligation to others? How can you spread your energy and your love around?

◆ *What do you want to say to your group about what you learned? How can you continue to move in this direction, following through on insights gained? Do you want to find others with whom to connect more regularly?*

I hope you are more comfortable with yourself and your new definition of success. I believe we can all achieve and grow as we desire once we let go of those things that hold us back; then we can open to our inner wisdom and use it to move beyond any obstacles that may be in the way.

Author's Final Note:

I am so very grateful to you for taking the time to participate in these Projects. I have enjoyed creating them for you. As I put them together, I experienced great joy getting material onto the computer and then imagining you working through the exercises—and coming into more of your special power and unique essence.

I hope to encounter you again, but I want you to know that whether I do or not, I appreciate and respect you . . . and I trust that you will go on to discover more and more of *your Inner Magic.* The power that we carry forward is important to our country and our world. May we all do our best to carry ourselves and the world to a better space.

Peace.

Bibliography

Adams, Kathleen, *Journal to the Self*, New York: Warner Books, Inc., 1990.

Arrien, Angeles, *The Four-Fold Way*, New York: HarperCollins, 1993.

Benson, M.D., Herbert, *The Break-Out Principle*, New York: Scribner, 2004.

Bridges, William, *Transitions; Making Sense of Life's Changes*, The Perseus Books Group, 1980.

Cameron, Julia, *The Artist's Way*, New York: Jeremy P. Tarcher/Putnam, 1992.

Cameron, Julia, *The Right to Write*, New York: Jeremy P. Tarcher/Putnam, 1998.

Capacchione, Lucia, *The Power of Your Other Hand*, Franklin Lakes, New Jersey: Franklin Press, 2001.

Choquette, Sonia, *Your Heart's Desire,* New York: Random House, Inc., 1997.

Covey, Stephen, *Seven Habits of Highly Effective People*, New York: Simon and Schuster, 1989.

Hanh, Thich Nhat, *Peace is Every Step,* New York: Bantam Books, 1991.

Hawkins, David, *Power vs. Force,* Carlsbad, CA: Hay House, Inc. 1995.

Lark, Susan, "The Lark Letter" quoting the Institute of HeartMath, www.heartmath.com, Potomac, MD: Healthy Directions, LLC.

Levine, Stephen, *Who Dies?,* New York: Anchor Books, 1982.

Levine, Stephen, *Guided Meditations, Explorations and Healings,* New York: Doubleday, 1991.

Levine, Stephen, *A Year to Live,* New York: Random House, Inc., 1997.

Myss, Carolyn, *Why People Don't Heal and How They Can,* New York: Random House, Inc. 1997.

Myss, Carolyn, *The Energetics of Healing* (video), Boulder, CO: Sounds True, Inc., 1997.

Nelson, G. Lynn, *Writing and Being,*

Northrup, M.D., Christiane, "Health Wisdom for Women" newsletter, Phillips Publishing, International, 800-211-8561. 2004.

Progoff, Ira, *At a Journal Workshop*, New York: Jeremy P. Tarcher/Putnam, 1975.

Rainer, Tristine, *The New Diary,* New York: Jeremy P. Tarcher/Penguin, 1978.

Silva, Jose, *You, the Healer*, Tiburon, CA: H J Kramer Inc., 1989.

Tillich, Paul, *Dynamics of Faith,* New York: Harper & Row, 1957.

Tolle, Eckhart, *Stillness Speaks*, Novato, CA: New World Library, 2003.

Wilbur, Ken, *A Brief History of Everything*, Boston, MA: Shambhala Publications, Inc., 1996.

CPSIA information can be obtained at www.ICGtesting.com
Printed in the USA
LVOW112124080812

293583LV00004B/112/A